MOTH CATCHER

Moth Catcher

An Evolutionist's Journey
Through Canyon and Pass

MICHAEL M. COLLINS

University of Nevada Press

RENO ❧ LAS VEGAS

This book was made possible in part by a generous grant
from the Nevada Biodiversity Initiative.

University of Nevada Press, Reno, Nevada 89557 USA
Copyright © 2007 by University of Nevada Press
All rights reserved
Manufactured in the United States of America
Design by Kathleen Szawiola

Library of Congress Cataloging-in-Publication Data
Collins, Michael M., 1943–
Moth catcher : an evolutionist's journey through canyon
and pass / Michael M. Collins. — 1st ed.
p.   cm.
Includes bibliographical references and index.
ISBN 978-0-87417-725-1 (hardcover : alk. paper) —
ISBN 978-0-87417-735-0 (pbk. : alk. paper)
1. Collins, Michael M., 1943– 2. Naturalist—United States—
Biography. 3. Saturniidae—Hybridization. I. Title.
QH31.C57A3 2007
595.78092—DC22
[B]   2007011377

The paper used in this book is a recycled stock made from
50 percent post-consumer waste materials and meets the
requirements of American National Standard for Information
Sciences—Permanence of Paper for Printed Library
Materials, ANSI/NISO Z39.48-1992 (R2002). Binding materials
were selected for strength and durability.

FIRST PRINTING
16 15 14 13 12 11 10 09 08 07
5 4 3 2 1

For Jane, Norah, Andrew, and Faith

METAMORPHOSIS

Today my father spoke to me
In a language I could understand, finally

This man whose tongue would spout
The Latin words I could do without:
Hyalophora, Cecropia, Ceanothus
In daughter's terms: some ole silk moths

This man who as a boy of fourteen
Published a book on moths it would seem
What once intimidated and haunted me
My father consumed with being scholarly

Today he spoke to me with words that I
Read through a tear filled eye
Recalling his youth, some words he penned
Words that even I could comprehend

This man I rattled like a cocoon
And caused his hair to white too soon

Now inspired and with renewed affection
After reading through his work of youthful reflection

For this man finally spoke to me in a language I did speak
And out of the cocoon the boy did peek

In the eyes of the daughter the father was finally seen
As a boy collecting caterpillars on the side of the stream

NORAH COLLINS CLINE

Spring 2002

CONTENTS

ILLUSTRATIONS

COLOR PLATES *(after page 76)*

PREFACE

ALL NATURALISTS are bewitched by a special creature, often one familiar from their youth and possessing an allure not defined by any formal taxonomic rank, separate from any research question, and more basic than beauty or size or popular reputation. We know early on that these animals strike an emotional note that we may never be allowed to describe in any terse research paper. We see them not as specimens but as creatures playing a role in nature, one that we devote ourselves to discovering and describing. For some it might be a cougar, a deer mouse, or Swainson's hawk. For me it was the cecropia moth and its western kin, especially the Rocky Mountain species, *Hyalophora gloveri*, an elegant burgundy wine-colored moth not well known among collectors. I could not have known how rewarding and challenging my early attraction to this group of species would become.

After filling a few specimen cases as a young collector, I discovered that I much more enjoyed field trips and raising moths and butterflies through their life stages. This experience taught me enduring lessons in natural history and ecology. The populations making up a species are not uniform, as the Latin name on a specimen label might imply, but often vary wonderfully over the species' range. Their wing patterns, the plants their caterpillars eat, even the parasites that attack them might each be different for a given region. Among the moths I raised, the *Hyalophora* species were not only especially striking in their size and beauty, but were also easy to hybridize in cages. As I began making cross-matings and rearing hybrids, I started to wonder how various traits were inherited, why female hybrids were sterile yet normal and vital otherwise, what their ancestor looked like, and how the several species arose. My early enchantment with the various *Hyalophora* species was a happy choice because they also happen to be among the relatively few Lepidoptera groups that hybridize in the wild. In some cases the species hybridize only rarely, but other combinations interbreed freely where their ranges overlap. By this measure, the various forms seem to be just on the borderline of evolving into full species. I became fascinated with these wild hybrid populations, all many hundreds of miles from my Midwest home, and saw them as natural laboratories where I might be able to study the origin of species.

The tick of the evolutionary clock is produced by the mechanism of speciation, the ultimate source of biodiversity. The wild silk moths revealed to me that evolution is not just a historical event lost in the deep past, such as the fall of the dinosaurs and the rise of the mammals. Species change and evolve even within our lifetimes. To understand the origin of biodiversity, and to hope to preserve it, we must understand how species form.

The June following my graduation from high school I took a field trip to the Rocky Mountains with my camping buddy Keith Erickson (fellow science fair competitor and future public health official), and we used female cecropia moths to lure in male *gloveri*. Perhaps the *gloveri* moth's most alluring quality was its home among distant, shrouded peaks and the lush canyons they preside over. This creature became my guide, from Arizona to the Canadian Rockies, in travels and studies to understand a story of evolution and speciation: the recolonization of the West at the close of the Pleistocene by the ancestors of these moths and how they adapted and became new species in a new landscape.

I began this book as an essay to help my grown children better understand how growing up in my time in the Midwest led to my fascination with nature. As the project developed, it grew in scope beyond a personal remembrance and I found myself writing a book. I have followed a narrative theme of personal discovery of the natural history of western mountains and canyons, some of which I relate in a descriptive and less personal manner. Canyons and mountain passes have played a role in the evolution and speciation of many organisms, including the wild silk moths I have studied, and so provide a natural pathway, literally and symbolically, to the more philosophical topics I present in the concluding chapters.

Transcribing my thoughts and experiences required introspection and effort, but the process was rewarding. If the result is partly an exercise in self-indulgence, at my age I can be excused for the pleasure in recounting fond memories; and if my children still don't fully understand their dad's eccentricities, I hope they and other readers will come to share my love of the western mountains, canyons, and deserts, and the intellectual and philosophical questions for which the wild silk moths are a metaphor.

ACKNOWLEDGMENTS

THIS BOOK began life as a collection of unpublished essays, where it languished for a time and might still had not my wife Pat lovingly pushed me to climb up the slope out of this sheltering canyon of private and personal memories and write a book with a wider perspective and outlook. With her keen sense of tone and texture in written language, she read through early drafts and weeded out many a rhetorical excess and bushy phrase. I am very grateful to Mindy Conner, who has nurtured this project from its early stages to final copyediting.

Following Mindy's suggestions to improve an early draft, I accepted her offer to introduce me to the University of Nevada Press, where the manuscript found a natural and happy home among so many respected titles in Great Basin history and natural history. From the outset, my editors Margaret Dalrymple and Sara Vélez expressed a genuine enthusiasm for the project, and I am very grateful for their faith in my concept of a book with such varied narrative themes—part personal memoir and part scientific exposition. Their expert guidance during revision and editing much improved the book. Working with the production and marketing staff was a pleasure as I watched the project take on its own life as writing ended and production began.

Writing a natural history work for a non-specialist audience was new to me, and I thank the many friends who volunteered to critique parts of or the entire draft. I thank especially Don Adams, Lincoln Brower, Ron Hodges, Margie Miller, Susanne Olive, John Rawlins, and old field trip friends Tom Ackerman, Keith Erickson, and Bob Weast. Bob Pyle and an anonymous reviewer critically annotated the manuscript, which improved both its content and clarity and my writing skills. I thank them all sincerely. Sincere thanks also to Gail Damskey of Raven's Eye Graphics who skillfully translated my hand drawings of gene frequency clines and phylogenetic trees into professional illustrations. Cam Sutherland drew the map of Monitor Pass and patiently rendered my crude sketch of a canyon into a clear and attractive figure. I thank also Peter Brussard, representing the Nevada Biodiversity Initiative, for partially funding the color plate expenses.

MOTH CATCHER

CHAPTER ONE

Indian Creek Memories

I REMEMBER many years ago watching a comedy skit performed by the Duck's Breath Mystery Theater in San Francisco that included the line "University of Ohio, Iowa City, Idaho." Those of us raised in the central region of the United States sometimes endure a coastal provincialism, but our memories let us face this good-natured taunting with a certain smugness of our own. When hearing where I grew up, people often admit they imagine Iowa as a monotony of tilled land somewhere in the Midwest. If they indulge me, I tell them I remember rolling wooded hills sloping into verdant fields, the exciting rush of spring following the crackling ice and silent snowscapes of winter, the symphony and drama of summer thunderstorms, and the soft pastel brushwork of fall. I spent much of my childhood alone, hiking and exploring near my home in eastern Iowa. These were years rich in discovery of nature, but a single event probably began my lifelong interest in the wild silk moths I still study today.

One late fall afternoon, I believe in 1953, I was exploring behind my neighbor Erroll's greenhouse and noticed objects hanging from twigs of a small wild cherry tree. At first they looked like unfallen leaves, but each was attached by shiny threads. Must be silk, I thought. As I reached out and touched one, I realized it was some kind of cocoon. I cut them free with my pocketknife, smelled the sweet odor of the cherry wood, and put the cocoons in my coat pocket. Somehow I resisted cutting them open to investigate the thud each one made when shaken, and put them instead in a box in a screened-in porch, a winter storage place and favorite summertime room for midwestern families. The cocoons waited for spring, more patiently than most of us humans.

When warm weather finally came I casually glanced at the box and was startled to see a large moth resting on one cocoon. It didn't fly away and allowed me to put my face close to it. For the first time I saw those rich red-brown earth tones as it slowly and proudly fanned its velvety wings back and forth. How could this large creature emerge from such a small, tightly woven cocoon? Why did it so confidently remain clinging to the cocoon and not fly away as a butterfly would? What was the purpose and meaning of the exquisite detail in the wing pattern, with its bold lines and colors, delicate shadings, and those small false eyespots at the wing tips? With its furry body and deliberate movements, the moth seemed more like a small mammal than a darting insect.

My dad encouraged me to read about my discovery and tentatively identified the moth as a polyphemus, one more example of his astounding general knowledge! I soon found that it was actually a promethea moth (*Callosamia promethea*) of the family Saturniidae. Later, I did find a polyphemus cocoon on hazelnut, oddly only a few feet from the same wild cherry. I went on to find and rear all the midwestern silk moths, including the regal cecropia, the large purple-and-yellow imperial, and the little io, with yellow males and mottled wood-colored females, both with hind wing eyespots they revealed when startled. No one forgets their first sight of the luna, exquisitely sculptured in green with long, curving tails, a creature that looks almost out of place in the familiar American landscape, as if it were part of another natural culture—Asian, perhaps—its evolutionary point of origin. While each was a moment of discovery, that first awakening to the promethea is still my most vivid memory.

※

I SOON DISCOVERED that cocoons could not be found on every bush but were scattered over vast areas in small clumps. Many of those I found produced flies and wasps—parasites whose larvae fed on the caterpillar and ultimately killed it. Birds and countless insect enemies feasted on the young caterpillars, so that only a tiny portion of the hundreds of eggs laid by a female were able to mature and produce moths each generation. (On average, in a stable population, only two will survive, replacing the female and her mate.) In nature, life is hard and uncertain for an individual, but species survive.

Through reading and rearing, I learned that these widely scattered moths reproduce by means of a chemical communication system. The female releases a scent, a pheromone, in minuscule amounts imperceptible to our noses. Carried by the wind, the pheromone is detected by the feathery antennae of the male, which responds by flying upwind and somehow finds the female through a maze of hills, trees, branches, and brambles. Most species fly at night or just before dawn. I would awaken at three or four in the morning to watch cecropias appear ghostlike in the dim light and sail gracefully over the porch where I had been sleeping, and then flutter gently toward the caged female I had reared the summer before. Sometimes four or five males would appear at once, yet a person could spend years looking during summer days and never find even one moth resting in concealment.

These moths were rare by insect standards, and yet they existed not as individuals but in a population tied together by their pheromone mating system. They were controlled in number by their enemies and by the hazards of weather, and distributed according to the abundance of the particular plants suitable for the caterpillars to eat. During the night, females found and identified these plants, an activity I could watch only briefly after releasing them because they soon flew out of sight. After a few days the moths would die. Unlike nectar-feeding butterflies, saturniid adults do not eat; stored fat is their only source of food. I mounted and preserved a few newly hatched adults; I bred many and watched them become tattered after mating and egg laying, and then die in confinement; and often I released others to chance their fate in the wild. These years were filled with lessons that both trained me in the science of ecology and helped me develop a philosophical understanding of the cycle of life.

JUST BEFORE an Iowa dawn in midsummer the air is still and heavy with humidity. The horizon is hidden in a soft mist; green hills blend into gray sky. The thick, humid air carries a mixed bouquet of summer smells: the scent of sweet clover and basswood in bloom, the nut-sweet odor of cut grass, and the musty smell of decaying wood and humus. An old green Studebaker pickup began slowly winding up our long, curvy driveway and quietly came to a stop. While the rest of the family slept, I ran down the brick walkway and jumped in. Irv had trained me not to disrespectfully slam the old girl's door. I remember the pleasing whine of the transmission as we started off for a day working with his bees.

During the week Irv was a senior draftsman in my dad's electronics company, but on the weekends he tended apiaries scattered around the county on several farms. Hearing of my interest in moths, Irv rekindled his similar boyhood hobby, when he and the Nissen brothers (of trampoline fame) collected and raised cecropia, luna, and other wild silk moths in Cedar Rapids in the 1930s. Irv was a quiet and polite person, quick to smile and to laugh, but never at the risk of giving offense. He reaffirmed my hope that an interest in "bugs"

was not clinically strange. I was grateful for his companionship in sharing a love for the outdoors, and he truly enjoyed
the chance to share his knowledge and enthusiasm (his own
children followed more conventional pursuits).

We would stop along country roads to look for caterpillars
during the summer, or for cocoons in the fall. Irv taught me
how two people can run along a railroad track, each holding
one end of a branch, leaning outward, and pulling against
the other's weight. The trick to maintaining this equilibrium is to keep your footing on the rail. Railroad and power
line right-of-ways are good places to collect because they are
sanctuaries from the plow and insecticide sprayer, and support a second growth of small trees and shrubs.

On cool mornings, especially in early summer, the wax
sealing the boxes, or "supers," of the hive was hard and made
a loud crack when we tried to pry the supers apart. This really upset the bees, and I always hoped I had tucked the netting
of my veil in around my neck! But I learned how to use dry
leaves to stoke the smoker and pump its bellows to calm the
bees. I found that if I relaxed and used slow, careful movements, the bees would allow us to remove the honey-laden
frames and add new ones, each with a wax sheet prestamped
with a hexagon pattern. Upon every hexagon the workers

would build the cells the hive uses to store honey and raise the brood.

Early spring honey made from dandelion nectar is bitter. You must wait until midsummer, when the bees visit the sweet clover, for sweet honey. We stopped to talk to the farmers, who were glad to see Irv; his bees ensured that the clover in the field and apple trees in the orchard would be pollinated. The bees track the seasons, selecting a sequence of flowers and raising new workers. Eventually, when the colony's numbers have increased to a certain level, a group swarms to form a new hive. I learned that newly hatched queens must escape the sting of the old queen, who tries to kill her rivals, and fly out to mate with the otherwise useless drones. As the size of the hive increases, workers brood more queen cells (by feeding royal jelly to the larvae). Eventually they raise more virgin queens than the reigning queen can vanquish. This competitive equilibrium between the existing queen and the workers sets limits on the size of the hive and ensures that the colony will reproduce during bountiful summers. These insects have their own complex society, separate from ours but interdependent with our agriculture. I came to appreciate that we are as much a part of nature as the bees are a part of our existence.

At noon we sometimes stopped to eat bag lunches along a cool creek bank, or in the fall to join farmers in a small-town café. I listened to their farm talk and especially to the jokes (never called gossip) they told about one another. I usually ordered a roast beef sandwich served open-faced on pure white Wonder Bread, with gravy and mashed potatoes on the side and perhaps a Jell-O salad on iceberg lettuce.

Irv always kept track of time and delivered me home before dark. With luck I carried with me a big imperial moth caterpillar on a box elder branch or, in late fall, a pocketful of promethea cocoons. The lore and lessons I learned from these outings eventually found their way into the moth books I would write.

OUR HOUSE was on the slope of a steep hill on thirteen acres, half divided between woods in the back and an immense lawn surrounding the house and maintained by weekly mowing during the summer. The "timber," as our housekeeper Gertie referred to it, was rich in tree species and home to a surprising array of creatures. Sugar maple, shagbark hickory, American elm, basswood (linden), ash, black walnut, white oak, and red oak formed a mature forest with a spreading canopy. Small ash trees from wind-blown seeds competed for light with the seedlings of the mature hardwoods. In the spring, as leaf buds were opening, a bloom of eager herbs and wildflowers relished the interlude of warm, wet weather and abundant light on the forest floor; within a week or two lush new canopy leaves would shade the sun, and the jack-in-the-pulpit, May apple, and other flowers would have matured and begun ripening their seeds. In more open areas, wild black cherry, box elder (actually a maple), and wild plum grew, in some places marking the boundary of old cultivation along fencerows. All this plant life was rooted in Iowa's famous dirt.

I can still remember my grade school teacher reading Laura Ingalls Wilder's *Little House on the Prairie*, with its description of the deep, dark loam of the Iowa prairie. Much of this soil is "loess" blown in by Ice Age winds from areas of glacial till—a mixture of sand, gravel, granite flour, and soil pushed in front of glaciers and freed by meltwater some ten thousand years ago. Organic matter was added through centuries of growth-and-decay cycles as the climate oscillated, at times favoring tall, lush prairie grasses, and at other times promoting woodland. In a climate of long, cold winters and hot, wet summers, the delicate balance of growth versus decay favored the accumulation of this black earth. In some places it was six feet thick before cultivation and erosion reduced it. The growth force stored in this soil seems in early summer to push its way up through trunk and stem to extrude vivid green leaves.

I learned to recognize most of the native birds, in spite of my zealous fascination with the big moths, and most revered the circling broad-winged hawks (their red-tailed cousins preferred land to the west) and the barred owls (close relatives of the loved/maligned spotted owl). I practiced a rather convincing imitation of the owl calls and entertained my family's dinner guests by inducing a forest denizen to return my evening salutation. Fox, rabbit, groundhog, raccoon, and an occasional deer lived in my neighborhood.

The property across the road was kept fallow by the neighbors who owned it and had long since reverted to native grasses and shrubs. It was a virtual paradise for a young naturalist and would today be a priceless refugium of native prairie plants and animals. My most vivid memory is of great spangled fritillary and tiger swallowtail butterflies feeding on thistles. A few gems sparkle in my memories, not just for their visual drama but also for their symbolism in connecting plant and creature. Once or twice I found the larvae of the giant swallowtail on prickly ash, a shrub related to citrus whose fruit was at first suggestive of oranges and then would prickle and tingle your lips and mouth. I confess I tricked friends into this taste test, but a softer memory is that of rearing the bird dropping–mimicking caterpillars into bright yellow-and-brown giant butterflies. A prize among collectors in the 1950s, these lovely animals now are considered pests in southern California and Tucson, Arizona, where they have colonized ornamental and agricultural citrus plantings.

In the fall I would search for cocoons, on wild plum and box elder trunks for cecropia and in the wild cherry groves for promethea, which I would then sell to teachers or collectors and sometimes trade for "exotic" eastern species. In my senior year in high school these fields were scraped clean, and a sterile housing subdivision now covers the land. How far, I wonder, must the children of this neighborhood today walk to enrich their lives with such experiences? Or could they?

※

ON A SUMMER'S EVENING I would set off barefoot for Erroll's house. I often began by walking up the hill behind our house to inspect the 156 small trees I had planted as forage for my hungry caterpillars. I remember the wind in the guy wires and elements of the large antennas my dad had installed in connection with his work. The hawks appreciated the view from this perch, as I did after climbing a few rungs on the masts. I walked downhill past the mesh sleeves protecting my luna larvae on walnut branches and heard the first nighthawk of the evening. A limestone wall banked the soil away from our long driveway, following the contour of the hill below our house. This was home to generations of chipmunks and was planted along its length with iris. In early summer these plants hosted hovering hummingbird moths, especially the white-lined sphinx (*Hyles lineata*), which visited the flowers at dusk ("hummingbird moths" refers to the hovering flight of the adult while sipping nectar; "sphinx" refers to the posture of the caterpillar at rest). At the bottom of the hill I preferred a route that took me along a short stretch of dusty unpaved road where I could feel between my toes the powder that was once limestone, and long before that an ancient Devonian seabed. This short contemplation always drew me out of the self-centered preoccupation of early teens and was somehow comforting.

Along Indian Creek Road I would lean over to smell the foliage of willow and poplar in the shallow ditch that collected runoff from the asphalt. Every summer I harvested a few viceroy butterfly larvae here, always leaving some to monitor during evening walks. Like the unrelated swallow-tail larvae, they independently invented the trick of looking like bird droppings, which fooled both birds and most adults I showed them to.

As I began walking down the curve of the Millers' drive on this night, I remembered my mother telling me that the first time she came visiting, Ella was busy mixing and pouring cement for the drive while Erroll was in the kitchen of their new house painting images of herbs and spices on the cabinet doors. They were not the conformist couple supposed to have typified the 1950s. I looked forward to dinners with them.

I would often see Erroll in the large garden, stooping over to cut zucchini and add them to the temptation of toma-toes and sweet corn he had already harvested. On the way back to the house I would inspect the door frame on the old chicken coop to see if the resident tree frog was still resting there, cryptic even against the gray, unpainted wood. Earlier in the summer he had emerged from the tadpole pond a few yards away.

The charcoal glowing, we began sizzling the steaks and drinking cokes, Erroll's with bourbon and mine without. I still remember the Millers' kitchen for its savory odors and the feel of the cool air as I descended the cellar stairs toward the shelves of canned vegetables. In summer they would make homemade tomato sauces and catsup from herbs and vegetables picked minutes before from their garden. Cooked slowly in large pots, this delicious brew made a mockery of the all-American condiment sold in stores. At a time when California-grown frozen vegetables were just becoming available, the Millers still canned fruits and vegetables that they stored in the storm cellar to add variety to winter meals. The Depression was a fresh memory for the Millers' generation, and it prompted them to stock up for lean times.

On springtime walks Erroll and I were sometimes lucky enough to find morels. Erroll would soak these rare mushrooms in salt water to drive out the tiny larvae of fungus gnats that sometimes shared this delicacy (and still do, though unnoticed, in wild morels sold seasonally in Midwest stores!) and then sauté them carefully in butter—but not with wine, which simply was not a household staple in those times. For the entrée we did eat our share of beef, but long before it became the West Coast vogue Erroll taught me the then-unappreciated delicacy of lamb shanks. One had to ask the butcher to save this cut, which was considered too bony and sinewy for T-bone-conditioned midwesterners.

Over dinner I would enjoy Erroll's stories of the tropics, of sights and sounds in the rain forests of Trinidad and Jamaica. "There are so many species of insects that you can't find a leaf without a hole chewed in it. I found out the hard way that I couldn't use watercolors and leave the picture out to dry. The ants would eat the paint, and the fungus and humidity would make the pages of my tablet stick together. And the wonderful beetles! Why don't you study beetles, Mike?" I reminded him of the luna moths we both loved. He would sprinkle in jokes and wordplay, and we would laugh at our private codes—hed-redded poodwecker, or my name as Ekim Snilloc—and Ella would chuckle and scold us for not acting our respective ages. Although well educated and a world traveler, she portrayed herself as a simple farmer on their "sand patch." (Their property was located on an old floodplain separated from Indian Creek by a small bluff.)

To my further prodding for stories Erroll would add a few about leading his company of Sea Bees (an acronym for Construction Battalion—Erroll held a degree in engineering) in the navy, but would become introspective and then quiet as his memories reached back to Guam and Tinian, only some ten or fifteen years back at that time. Landing a few days after the initial invasion, he met a group of marines just returning from the front line of battle, their dirty uniforms blotched with their own and others' dried blood. Embarrassed at his clean uniform, Erroll rubbed dirt on his pants and on the shiny holster of his .45 automatic. At the remains of a Japanese bunker he found a small lacquered box, beautifully carved and inlaid with a floral design, but scored through by some GI's knife or bayonet. Erroll didn't have to point out to me these contradictions of the Japanese culture, or the anger of the marine who first found the box.

Ella (also known as "Johnnie" for Ella Johnson Miller or, during disputes, as "The Warden") would add a story or two about working in a munitions factory making fuses for artillery shells. Like many of her generation, she was liberated by wartime opportunity and responsibilities, but unlike many she maintained an unfeminine role as a community leader and did her share of masculine chores. I began to appreciate the force of history that had shaped their lives, and eventually to understand why they drank perhaps a bit too much as a balm to their disappointments and frustrations. I was in some ways their only child, and their friendship at first soothed my sorrow at losing my mother and later, but perhaps precociously, provided genuine adult companionship.

At the end of the evening, I walked across their lawn to feel the grass wet with dew, my steps sometimes punctuated by a succulent night crawler. As I stepped onto the still-warm asphalt, I glanced back at their house and saw the yellow-green traces of lightning bugs flashing their coded mating signals across the lawn. By now the moon lit the way, and I knew the path well. I had to check on my caged polyphemus moth to see if she had drawn in any males. I fell asleep on the porch to sounds of katydids and crickets and thunder in the distance.

⚜

ERROLL'S RECIPE for mint sauce for lamb shanks:

In a saucepan add a tablespoon of wine vinegar to a quarter cup of red wine (wine was lacking in Erroll's original sauce; I use a rich cabernet, not a cheap cooking wine) and a quarter cup of sweet clover honey (my contribution). With experience, dilute with water to taste; the final product should be a sauce, not syrup. Simmer at very low heat until the sauce

FACING PAGE:

The Millers personified the midwestern virtues of self-reliance, intellectual curiosity, and a deep connection with nature. Erroll in his greenhouse, circa 1959. Ella and the author in 1982. Courtesy Brenda Campbell.

begins to thicken as water evaporates; add three or four sprigs of garden-fresh mint.

&

ALEX LIPPISCH had dark, deep-set eyes shining beneath a high forehead and thinning hair combed straight back—an intimidating appearance until you engaged him in conversation. Then he would flash displays of intense interest, concentration, and delight. You knew in a moment that he was extremely intelligent, but he was always courteous and genuinely interested in what you had to say. Alex held a doctorate in aeronautical engineering and by a twist of fate worked for the Messerschmitt aircraft company during World War II, where he designed the ME 163 rocket-powered fighter. Many jet fighters of the 1950s and 1960s—and more recently the supersonic Concorde—used this plane's pioneering delta-wing design. Alex worked for my dad helping to integrate flight control instruments and systems with different airframes. At a time when the nation was looking to Wernher von Braun to help counter the Russian rocket menace, Lippisch was *our* German scientist in Cedar Rapids.

His devotion was flight as a natural phenomenon, whether

practiced by man or mosquito. Alex and his sons could sit down at their workbench and in minutes cut out balsa wood pieces and assemble an ornithopter of their own design. Wound up with a rubber band, a small crankshaft would spin and flap the hinged wings via levers. The wonderful craft would flap its way around the yard, so light that unseen breezes would loft it over hummocks and around obstructions. Alex would lose himself in the spectacle and with childlike joy and waving arms gently shout encouragement and directions to his creation: "Yah, Yah—up, up—Yah goot," laughing as it seemingly obeyed his commands.

I remember listening to him play the lute during Sunday visits while I ate wursts, dark bread, and cheeses with exotic names and tastes. His wife, Gertrude, taught Renaissance history at the local college. Their sophisticated Continental interests and demeanor were not expressions of a longing for Europe and its recent tragic past. They thrived in their converted farmhouse and property along Indian Creek. Alex delighted in the friendly openness and lack of pretense of the American Midwest and was proud of his U.S. citizenship. He loved to recount Sid Caesar's television skit of the dresser adorning his employer with braid and medals, punctuated by their phonetic imitation of German (a Sid Caesar talent), whereupon the "officer" opened a door and blew a cab whistle at the entrance to a grand hotel!

I still have the *Field Guide to Insects* by Frank Lutz that Alex gave to me in 1954. He was always eager to help me in my budding natural history interests and told me of collecting moths and butterflies in Germany as a child. Sometime about 1958 Alex began filming episodes for a local television show called *Secrets of Flight.* I had been collecting post-Christmas poinsettias on which to rear the caterpillars of a sphinx moth (*Erynnyis ello*) sent to me by a friend in Florida. When the moths began emerging a few weeks later, Alex called me. Could I spare one of the moths to use in his program? One evening I met Alex and a photographer and watched intently as they set up a Mitchell high-speed camera. Their hope was to film the hovering flight of the hummingbird moth, and perhaps one of its quick dashes from flower to flower. But the moth eyed us suspiciously as we confined it in a glass box, turned on bright lights, and naively coaxed it to fly. I wonder if it could process the image of three pairs of round vertebrate eyes staring at it. In any event, it made a mad dash for freedom, never bothering to grace us with a hover, but in the process zipping past the lens just long enough to capture an image, lasting only an *Augenblick*. I had promised Alex a stellar performance and was crushed that my ungrateful moth, which I had raised free from enemies on well-watered houseplants, failed to live up to its billing.

I wish I could revisit Alex now and show him the film others have since made of hummingbird moths, swimming through the air with flexing wings trapping the air and expelling it in a complex circular motion I know he could explain. The thermoregulation and metabolism that regulate hummingbird moth flight have been studied as a model of natural bioengineering. Heat energy from flight muscles is trapped in the thorax, raising the muscle tissue to its most efficient temperature; the moth's body fluids carry away the excess heat. The nectar diet of these moths allows an energy-extravagant lifestyle that is denied to the nonfeeding and slower-flying saturniids. What a conversation Alex and I could have.

❧

DURING MY SENIOR YEAR in high school I received a small book from my friend Bob Weast in Des Moines that profoundly shaped my perception of the natural world and my formal studies in biology. Bob was a close friend, a professor of music at Drake University, and a fellow moth enthusiast.

We had just coauthored a small natural history guide to the wild silk moths when he sent me an extra copy of W. R. Sweadner's monograph on the evolution of the cecropia moth and its close relatives. I had by this time broadened my view of the natural world beyond "stamp collecting" specimens to an appreciation of species as collections of natural populations living in a certain way in a defined area, using life cycle adaptations to beat the odds of survival. But my concept of evolution was limited to the rise and fall over immense sweeps of time of major groups such as the dinosaurs. Sweadner's book introduced to me the concept that evolution also occurs at the much finer scale of speciation. Species evolve from earlier ancestral species. These daughter species evolve adaptations to new and changing environments. We recognize clusters of such closely related species as genera, and as this process of branching differentiation continues, families and higher taxonomic groups arise. Evolution is a process reflected in the tree of relationships referred to as a "phylogeny," and Sweadner's thesis attempted to explain the evolution of the cecropia group from a common ancestor. As a budding naturalist familiar with populations and geographic variation, I instinctively grasped the significance of Sweadner's study of speciation.

Sweadner described the effect that the Ice Age has had on all communities of organisms in North America. By a geological yardstick, the current distribution of plants and animals and the climate we live in are quite recent. The very ground I grew up on was once just south of a massive front of glaciers, and was only ten thousand years ago a windswept tundra devoid of trees. All plants and creatures in the northern states and Canada have only recently expanded into their current ranges and had to adapt to the new climate and environment they now inhabit.

Evidence for evolution can be found in the geographic variation within a species across its range, and in the distribution of closely related species as distinct geographic isolates, peripheral to the parent species. Such biogeographical evidence, termed "horizontal evolution" by Ernst Mayr, inspired Darwin in his formulation of evolution through natural selection. "Vertical evolution" is the story in fossils of the appearance of major groups of organisms and the extinction of others through geological time. Sweadner's work was in the horizontal realm.

Sweadner was an entomologist at the Carnegie Museum in Pittsburgh who specialized in Lepidoptera. He knew from his work at the museum that moths in the cecropia group—

four recognized species at that time—were distinct in color and pattern but lacked effective mating barriers. In a cage, males of one species would mate with females of another, producing offspring that were normal except that the female hybrids were sterile. In the Bitterroot Mountains of Idaho and Montana, moths in this group (the genus *Hyalophora*) appear intermediate between the Rocky Mountain *H. gloveri* and the West Coast *H. euryalus*. Sweadner reasoned from the geographic location of the Bitterroots, and from the lack of reproductive isolation, that this northwestern race was in fact a natural hybrid population. His thesis was that as the ice and glaciers retreated at the end of the Ice Age, the moths expanded their ranges from refugia to the south and followed their host plants northward as the climate warmed. The two species met in the region of the Bitterroots and hybridized.

Although it was stapled between drab cardboard covers, I found his treatise exciting. He described his solo expedition in the 1930s to the Bitterroots to collect these moths and the methods he used to quantify and analyze their wing patterns. Sweadner discussed their hybrid origin as an example of speciation in progress: the divergence of forms in all respects except the final stage of reproductive isolation that defines "good" species. By blind good fortune I had become entranced by a problem in evolutionary biology that was to become a hot topic in the 1970s: the study of natural hybrid zones as windows into the evolutionary process of speciation. His work drew me westward, to the mountain and desert regions I had earlier visited, and the creatures hidden in their canyons.

CHAPTER TWO

Into the Canyon

IN EARLY SUMMER OF 1961, while Keith and I were on our moth-trapping venture, I learned that I had been accepted by the University of California at Berkeley. I had camped and collected moths on a few occasions in the Rocky Mountains and in Arizona, but the Great Basin, Sierra Nevada, and West Coast were familiar only through books. As fall approached I was eager to leave the Midwest, to trek two thousand miles across the continent and begin life as a college student in the San Francisco Bay area. With steady driving I could reach Colorado, my personal frontier, in a day and a half.

From Iowa you must drive across Nebraska and eastern Colorado to reach the Rockies. As Interstate 80 crosses the Missouri River, a midwesterner's perception of topography is reset from "rolling hills" to "truly flat," although to a westerner the change might seem imperceptible. This stretch of plains—from moist tallgrass prairie to dry short-grass prairie—creates a yearning for the first sight of cloud-shrouded massifs and the steep-walled canyons that buttress them. In some of us the attraction is inbred and warmly primal.

I knew I would soon be walled in by tall campus buildings and the intensity and responsibility of study at Berkeley. That first drive across the West, and my subsequent fall and spring commutes, were times of mothing, musing, collecting, and contemplation of my fascination with mountains, canyons, and deserts. I was first drawn to canyons as a modern hunter-gatherer and probably followed the spark of ancient neuron networks as I drove up jeep trails into the canyons of desert and Great Basin ranges where I could find the best collecting and campsites. As I matured in my studies I began to see canyons as natural refuges, as dioramas of ancient climates and biological communities (revealed in stratified plant zones ascending mountain slopes), and as theaters of natural drama played out over the seasons. My earliest experiences were in the Sonoran Desert of Arizona.

❦

THE MOUNTAIN RANGES of southeastern Arizona are islands in the desert. Their slopes cool and condense moisture-laden air from the Gulf of Mexico during the late-summer monsoon season. In spectacular thunderstorms, rain drenches the mountain slopes and finds its way to gullies that channel runoff into canyon bottoms; creeks form in minutes, then swell into rushing streams that flood arroyos and fan water over the desert floor. In an hour or two the drama is over, but you can feel the humidity rise as the sun and warm earth evaporate the runoff and thirsty plants reluctantly transpire countless gallons of precious water.

Without such rains the Sonoran Desert would truly be a barren and uncertain place. Because of the yearly monsoons, a resplendent diversity of plants and animals find refuge in these mountains, partitioned into an array of life zones from creosote scrub on the desert floor to saguaro cactus forests on lower slopes to oak woodland at middle elevations to mountaintop conifer forests. The canyons, especially, beckon both desert travelers and wildlife with running creeks and sycamore shade. The weathered mountains in the Southwest look old, and indeed they are, but the desert community and climate are quite recent in geological time.

During cooler and wetter Ice Age times, plant and animal colonizers from the mountains of Mexico invaded this entire region. They are now confined to their preferred zone in a mountain sanctuary, surrounded by inhospitable desert. Madrone growing in the Santa Ritas has its closest relative in the *madroño* trees of the Sierra Madre. Birdwatchers trek to Madera Canyon hoping to see a Mexican trogon in the species' northernmost outpost.

Studies of pack rat middens—the heap of nest materials and discarded seeds that accumulate over countless generations of use by these inveterate homebuilders—show that the bottom layers are quite old; some have been dated to 40,000 years BP (before the present). Preserved seeds of pinyon and juniper, for example, are found in areas that now support mesquite and cactus. At one time, what is now Sonoran Desert was more like the pinyon-juniper country of the Great Basin. As the climate became warmer and drier, most of the pack rats' fellow creatures moved upslope, but the adaptable *Neotoma* remained to chronicle climate change in a language that biologists can decipher. Driving downslope along a canyon road in the Sonoran Desert can replay in space the climate change that occurred over thousands of years.

Madera Canyon, in the Santa Rita Mountains south of Tucson, had become in my imagination a legendary site where exotic Mexican saturniid moths and other creatures, perhaps even jaguars, could be seen. In the late 1950s no book catalogued the large moths of the Sonoran Desert region, but I knew from collectors and museum visits that in this corner of Arizona you could use an ultraviolet light to collect an astounding number and diversity of insects in a single night.

My first visit to Madera Canyon was during a rainy night in August 1959, at the peak of the monsoon, when the desert flora broadcast a rich, sweetly pungent odor. I could see the plant life change as I climbed in elevation, first across the bajada—the outwashed fan of rock rubble that accumulates over the ages at a canyon's mouth—and then into the canyon itself. The surrounding walls and peaks were only dim

FACING PAGE:

Entrance to Madera Canyon in the Santa Rita Mountains south of Tucson, Arizona. Old friend Bob Weast searches for caterpillars of *Eupackardia calleta* on the rain-induced foliage of ocotillo. Mesquite and other thorny legumes occur at this elevation (4,000 feet); Mexican blue oak and alligator juniper grow on the hillsides in the background.

Sycamore and silverleaf oak
along Madera Creek during
the late-summer monsoon season.

outlines, but I could sense their closeness funneling the car into the mountains. The air was quickly cooler, and light rain began to fall. Then, suddenly, large moths began flying across the road, mostly fast sphinx moths streaking by with red eyes glowing in the intense glare of the headlights. A few were larger and slower, but I couldn't be sure which silk moth they could be.

One February day, decades after my first visit, I returned to the Santa Rita Mountains. I had parked at the upper trailhead and hiked up Madera Canyon following the dry creek bed for a way, then left this trail and followed a game trail—made by far more agile creatures than I—diagonally up the canyon's south face to a small boulder beneath an oak where I found a flat spot to sit down and open my pack for lunch. I had discovered that I saw more if I was seen less, and I tried to keep my movements to a minimum. Here, in the shade of the oak, I could view the expanse of the ridgeline and the layering of vegetation on the opposite canyon wall, and I could look down the canyon to the desert below. This rocky cathedral, with its forest and scrub tapestry, drew my thoughts away from caterpillar hunting or any such preoccupation with detail. In the distance to the north rose the Santa Catalina Mountains. The air was surprisingly clear, and I could distinguish the dark

Gambel oak (6,000 feet) silhouetted against a pinyon-juniper-covered hillside in Madera Canyon; the desert floor is visible in the distance.

green of the pines and Douglas-fir near the peaks from the gray-green oak belt on the slopes below. Tucson was a giant amoeba spreading out into the foothills, probing the canyons and surrounding desert for favorable invasion routes. Seen as an abstract entity, it truly was an organism, taking in petroleum and water nutrients and expelling brownish gaseous waste. Its success and growth now threatened the very desert and mountains that brought people to it. I was glad to be in the solitude of the Santa Ritas.

The canyon soothed my somber preoccupation with man's threat to nature, and I lost myself in the portrait of the zones of vegetation. I tried to imagine the scope and pattern on the landscape of the animal populations confined to this canyon. Every year they have to pair up, reproduce, and entrust their fate as a species to the next generation. What was their connection to others of their kind in neighboring canyons? How often did they exchange visits and genes? Some of the less mobile species must be essentially isolated here. Do some species go extinct during exceptionally harsh winters or severely dry summers, here at the northern end of their range, to be replaced eventually by colonizers from Mexico? Some of the vertebrates, especially, must exist in relatively small numbers. What would this place have been like at the end of the Ice Age, only a moment ago by nature's clock?

Shocked from my reverie by a Mexican jay's cry, I sat up and stretched and began the slow walk back to the car. I like to hike canyons at various times of the day and over several seasons. Everything changes from one visit to the next—the color of the rocks; the bloom, growth, and senescence of the vegetation; the mix of birds and butterflies; even the other hikers and naturalists I meet. Spring courting and nest building are peak interest times for birders. On one trip a group of gregarious ladies put down their field glasses to engage me in conversation and were delighted that I was an expert on cecropia moths, which were familiar to the one from the Midwest ("back east" in western parlance).

Returning years later during the rainy season, I drove the truck up to the trailhead for the Carrie Nation Mine. The trail followed the creek bed, aside from one or two sections of switchbacks to gain altitude. Strictly out of habit I casually looked on the familiar California coffee berry for pale swallowtail caterpillars, a common western species but unrecorded from Arizona. Its absence here is a reminder that most of the Santa Ritas' flora and fauna are colonizers from Mexico. On coffee berry I was more likely to find the exquisite black-

and—lemon yellow (probably chemically protected) larvae of the saturniid *Agapema homogena*. I restrained myself (with a couple of exceptions) from clambering up rocky slopes to inviting clumps of *Ceanothus* where the *Hyalophora gloveri* were probably hiding. I didn't want to knock rocks down on the trail and bonk a tourist.

There weren't as many butterflies on the wing as there should have been, probably due to the late start of the monsoons. I saw a few of the unusually large local variety of two-tailed swallowtail (*Papilio multicaudatus*), which I had often photographed nectaring on thistle on other trips. The California sister (*Adelpha bredowii*) is also larger and even more colorful here in the Arizona mountains, and many were drinking from the stream bank, sucking in the dissolved salts they require.

I had lunch while sitting on a log, and after eating (not before, as advised by the Boy Scout handbook) I looked under the log. There was a Sonoran mountain kingsnake, a coral snake mimic, decked out in vivid red, white, and black, with the yellow-tipped nose typical of this subspecies. I gently prodded it with a stick to get it into good light and took several pictures while it moved in a slow, confident manner, poking this way and that into the sticks and grass for an escape from this large, annoying creature. As I walked back to the trail, a birder couple approached. I urged them to walk over to the log and inspect this rare reptile, whose numbers have been generally reduced throughout its range by overcollecting. Only fifteen feet away, they nevertheless reflexively snapped their field glasses to their eyes and scanned the area for the harmless little snake. Spying it, they still did not walk over to make its acquaintance. I wondered if they shopped at the supermarket in the same way.

I finally reached the old cabin, past the rusting hulk of a small steam boiler that was probably hauled up the canyon in pieces strapped to hapless mules or donkeys. The miners may have used it to remotely power a water pump down in the mine shaft. Farther up the trail, the view from the cabin was magnificent—in one direction to the high, pine-covered ridgeline, and in another down the canyon to the desert floor far below in the distance. I photographed an old madrone, the Madrean species (*Arbutus arizonica*), which is smaller than our Sierran form but stately and enduring. This one had large sections of dead, gray tissue and was nearly as gnarled and twisted as a Sierra juniper. Perhaps lightning had hit it. Just then thunder began booming from the peaks to the south, over which huge cumulous clouds were spilling and flowing down toward me. I headed back, caught my stride, and reached the truck just as the rain began to fall.

Early one September morning I left for Madera Canyon on a mission to find a certain leaf-eating creature that had eluded my collecting efforts for many years. I climbed over the fence that proscribed the "Southwest Range Experimental Area" (or some such euphemism) and stepped into an area not grazed down to rock and rubble. It was, in fact, lush in two-foot-tall grass from the previous month's rains, and in the first hours of morning the air actually felt humid. I hiked to nearby rocky slopes through thick stands of ocotillo, a shrub with long, whiplike branches splayed out from a base. These plants put out foliage only after sustained rain, and this season they were deep green with small leaves which, due to the open architecture of the plant, can collect sunlight at any angle throughout the day. The leaves barely conceal rows of sharp spines that most people know from photos of the plants in spring, when the tips of the bare branches display gaudy red blooms.

Much sooner than I expected I spied a section of branch completely defoliated for about two feet of its length, and even before reaching the spot I spotted the unlikely defoliator. The caterpillar of *Eupackardia calleta* (the "calleta moth"—it has no common name) sports colors that demand explanation in a land of subtle gray-greens, browns, and rusty hues (see plates 5 and 6). Its body is a vivid aqua blue–green splotched with black markings. The rows of spiny tubercles are electric blue with a coral red base, surrounded with creamy white. The true legs are orange-red and the false legs, or prolegs, are yellow. I was surprised to realize that at a distance the black markings did tend to break up the outline of the beast, but I soon found two more larvae on the same plant. At close range the caterpillars certainly looked aposematic, or warningly colored. My old friend Bob Weast had long ago observed that the tubercle spines break at the slightest touch and exude a bitter-tasting drop of fluid. Decades later a group of German biochemists analyzed this hemolymph (insect blood) and found a high concentration of toxic amines that are known to repulse vertebrates but are less effective against invertebrates. The fluid is also unusually high in sugars.

I have pondered their findings and have a theory that fits the pattern of the color and chemistry. The bright colors probably do warn birds that the larvae are toxic, but the sugars may actually attract ants. While ants are normally an enemy, certain butterfly larvae reward ants with sugar, and the ants in turn drive away wasps and parasitic flies that can kill the larvae. Perhaps the calleta caterpillars employ the same strategy here in the desert, where ants are certainly abundant. This theory remains to be tested by someone with time, patience, and a wide-brimmed hat.

Over the next few days I observed the larvae in captivity and noticed that they tracked the sun's movement by periodically crawling into the shade, over the course of the day eating leaves from all sides of the branch. The adult males are day flyers with dull black wings trimmed in red (see plate 7). They are unusually large for day-flying saturniid moths, and are in fact about the same size as the black adults of the pipevine swallowtail (*Battus philenor*), which is known to be distasteful to birds. In the East several species of butterflies are suspected to be mimics of the pipevine swallowtail, and perhaps in the Sonoran Desert calleta adults perform this role.

The cocoon of the calleta moth is easier to find than the larva, as it is chalky white and spun at the base of its host. In the winter these cocoons are only partially hidden by twigs and dry grass. This moth is much sought after by collectors, and in the 1980s I heard tales of busloads of Japanese lepidopterists traveling to Madera Canyon to collect them. More than literal truth, I suspect these stories likely represented the paranoia of "Japan, Inc." that prevailed at that time, but in any case natural populations of such insects are rarely threatened by overcollecting. Habitat destruction, such as through development or overgrazing, is their true nemesis.

If we could endow the moth with any power of expectation it would be that its environment not change faster than the ability of its genome to evolve appropriate adaptations. The chemical structure of DNA is so stable, and the replication process so faithful, that a continuity of descent links all life back to precell times when competing molecular systems were subject to natural selection for their ability to extract energy from the environment and to replicate themselves. Yet the bonds linking DNA base pairs are not so strong that mutation cannot occur, and in this way genetic variation arises.

Modern genetics, founded in molecules and mathematics, has reduced the mechanism of inheritance to its elemental units. In the abstract, organisms have been described as merely the vessels carrying a bag of interacting genes from one generation to the next. The Darwinian paradigm sees gene variants competing among themselves to establish which is the most adapted to the environment. This harsh, reductionist viewpoint should in no way degrade our appreciation of the majesty of life. Every species has a story to tell written in its genes that is partly revealed in its life history adaptations. So I revere the showy calleta caterpillar munching on ephemeral ocotillo leaves in Madera Canyon.

> I thought of the long ages past—of this little creature [king bird of paradise] living and dying amid these dark and gloomy woods, with no intelligent eye to gaze upon the loveliness—while on the other hand, should civilized man ever reach these distant lands, we may be sure that he will disturb the nicely balanced relations of organic and inorganic nature as to cause the extinction of these very beings whose wonderful structure and beauty he alone is fitted to appreciate and enjoy. This consideration must surely tell us that all living things were *not* made for man. (Alfred Russel Wallace, circa 1856 [Raby, 2001, p. 122])

CHAPTER THREE

A Short Natural History
of Canyons

HIKERS AND NATURALISTS are drawn to canyons for their promise of shade, water, and shelter, and to observe the plants and animals that seek these same resources. I am certain this attraction is deeply seated and instinctual, dating back to our hunter-gatherer genesis. Canyons in the southwestern states offer a microclimate—a range of microclimates, really—that is generally cooler and supports greener and lusher vegetation than the surrounding mountains and deserts or basins. Canyons have their own natural history, and the basis for their unique environment is surprisingly complex. They are the arenas for natural communities typically much more diverse than those just beyond their boundaries.

Canyons have their origin in the erosion that attacks mountains as soon as they begin to form. Regardless of whether mountains are formed by tectonic forces uplifting blocks of the earth's crust or by the catastrophic upheaval of volcanic activities, irregularities on sloping surfaces channel rainwater, increase its velocity, and carry in suspension abrasive particles ranging in size from sand to boulders. Erosion occurs at varying rates depending on rainfall and the slope, hardness, and cohesion of the exposed substrate, but even granite will succumb over the ages to the relentless forces of erosion.

The width and depth of a preexisting canyon generally increases during an ice age, both through higher precipitation during the warm and wet phases and in certain locales also by the action of glaciers and ice flows during the coldest phases. Yosemite's majestic valleys and cliffs are thought to have begun forming about sixty thousand years ago and to have finished with the retreat of the glaciers a mere ten thousand years ago. In addition to glacial ice sheets in northern latitudes, the Cascades, Sierra Nevada, and Rocky Mountains supported small glaciers, and the snow load carried by mountain ranges in general increased during periods of glacial maxima, when rates of snowfall greatly exceeded summer melt. The final melting of the ice fields and glaciers at the end of the Pleistocene was a period of severe erosion and flooding. The size and age of the Grand Canyon place it in a special category, but most other canyons in our region must surely have been shaped more by Ice Age erosion than by any erosion experienced since then.

Tectonic forces heaving and folding massive plates of the earth's crust tend to form mountains with a general geographic orientation, such as the north–south placement of Great Basin ranges and the Sierra Nevada of California. Our largest canyons therefore face more-or-less west on the western slopes, and east on the eastern slopes. Side canyons within them tend to be oriented north and south.

Exposure to the sun largely determines each canyon's mix of microclimates, on both large and small scales. North-facing slopes often support plant communities quite different from those found on south-facing slopes. In the Sierra foothills, conifers or oaks grow on the former while heat-tolerant chaparral covers south- and west-facing slopes. In canyons leading into the sea along the northern coast of California, towering redwoods dominate the north-facing walls. A short hike across the creek and up the south-facing slope takes you into a more open Douglas-fir forest. Near the ocean, though, summer fog extends inland and can provide enough moisture from condensation and drip to lessen the contrast in floral composition. All such contrasts in microclimate and plant community will be even more dramatic in steep-walled canyons, with their deeper, longer-lasting daily shade.

The air in valleys and basins expands as it is heated during the morning, creating upslope breezes in the canyons of adjacent mountains; in late afternoon this air cools and contracts, drawing down cooler replacement air from the higher altitudes. Narrow canyons funnel this airflow, often changing breezes into winds within their walls. On still nights, cool air drainage may occur, especially in large canyons leading from the high country down into the lowlands, so that the microclimate within the canyon will be much cooler than that on exposed open slopes.

The flow of water that originally formed a canyon leaves as its descendants creeks and streams whose flow varies seasonally—or may even cease altogether for part of the year— but which support a distinctive riparian plant community. Even in desert regions, canyon streams may be lined with cottonwood, sycamore, walnut, and ash trees not far from cactus and ocotillo on parched adjacent slopes. Shade from these trees and the cooling effect of their transpiration further accentuate the canyon's cooler microclimate.

Canyon walls expose multiple geologic strata of different

ages and composition, ranging from decomposed granite to sandstone to shale, for example. Differing innate erosion rates for each layer will in turn create an uneven or shelflike canyon wall. This structure of ledges and crevasses creates homes for local communities of plants and animals. Certain plants may be especially adapted to specific soil types (a fern on basic limestone or digger pine on serpentine rock, for instance). A porous layer overlying bedrock may store and channel groundwater, which appears as seeps, or springs, emerging from canyon walls.

The outwash of erosion forms a fan-shaped canyon mouth called a *bajada* in the Southwest. These alluvial fans are typically very rocky on steep slopes and change to sand and gravel as the slope levels out. Even boulders may litter the area as a result of flash floods or from torrents of water released at the end of glacial periods. In desert regions canyons lead into arroyos channeling through the bajadas; these are usually dry except during the rainy season. In the Great Basin and Rocky Mountains, where mountain snows release early summer meltwater, streams may lead away from canyons and meander for miles in sagebrush basins. A narrow band of willow and cottonwood often lines such waterways.

The complex array of plant communities within canyons

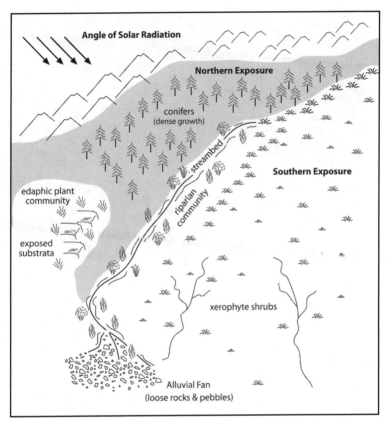

South-facing slopes are hotter and drier than north-facing slopes and support vegetation more tolerant of these conditions, such as chaparral. Broad-leafed trees and conifers (especially at higher altitudes) often blanket north-facing slopes.

Varied plant communities in Carson Canyon near Woodfords, Alpine Co., Calif., the western limit of the *Hyalophora* hybrid zone. Conifers cover the north-facing slope (*left*), while heat-tolerant shrubs such as manzanita and *Ceanothus* (*left and right foreground*) and bitterbrush grow on the south-facing slope (*right*). Poplar, willow, alder, and rose line the banks of the Carson River and follow it into the pinyon pine community.

attracts and supports a complementary diversity of ani-mals. Every shrub, tree, or herbaceous plant may be host to specific insects; their flowers attract specific pollinators; and their fruit and seeds nourish a certain collection of birds and mammals. The leaves of many plants contain one or more phytochemicals that protect them from general attack by herbivores. We know the effects of these plant compounds in terms of nicotine in tobacco, and more innocuously as the scents and flavors of herbs in our kitchens. Plants protected in this way are eaten only by specific insects that have evolved enzymes able to detoxify the noxious chemicals in the leaves, or in some cases to sequester them for the insect's own protection. As these adaptations are perfected through evolution, the same plant chemicals may even come to serve as an attractant aiding the female insect to locate and oviposit on the plant. Such life history adaptations relating to food chain, or trophic, links between organisms regulate the flow of energy within natural communities and give ecosystems structure and stability. (You can see why introduced weeds, lacking natural enemies, can be so disruptive and destructive.) The biodiversity that derives from these interactions is much more than a mere listing of plant and animal species.

Competition for a scarce resource is a theater for Darwinian selection. Population geneticists are drawn to these settings not to measure a struggle between individuals but to measure the frequency and fitness of genes. Along streambeds in the arid West, the soil water content drops off quickly with distance from the stream. Botanists in Utah found that the male and female box elders they studied differed in their ability to cope with drought. Male trees were more abundant away from the stream in Red Bluff Canyon near Salt Lake City, while female trees were more common near the stream. They concluded that differential mortality among seedlings was responsible for this distribution.

Genetic structuring of populations in response to environmental factors is common in nature. Well-studied examples include the increase in frequency of enzymes regulating alcohol tolerance in fruit flies near fermentation vats and a pattern of increased heavy metal tolerance in plants growing near mines. In all such cases strong natural selection favors a certain genotype within a species in a certain setting, but as the intensity of selection decreases away from these sites, the frequency of the gene also decreases. This clinal structuring is maintained in spite of the tendency of gene flow through dispersal to homogenize the population. (I return to the concept of gene frequency clines in chapter 6.) Such studies remind us that diversity, both within and among species, is a critical resource in nature.

As snowmelt from western mountains tapers off in midsummer, so does the flow of water in canyon streams, and the streams are no longer a dependable source of water. Using the fact that different concentrations of certain hydrogen isotopes occur in stream water and in the soil along stream banks, clever researchers found that mature trees in canyons don't take up water from the stream itself, but rather from deep down in the underlying soil. Seedlings depend on shallow surface moisture, while young trees are able to tap into the deeper stream water near banks. Mortality must be high in canyons where yearly precipitation varies greatly until trees reach a size where they can exploit the deeper soil moisture.

Some plants limit their growth and reproduction to the spring and early summer when soil moisture is still relatively high. Other plants have intrinsically more efficient molecular mechanisms that allow photosynthesis to proceed in spite of drought stress, and they continue to grow and develop seeds well into summer. Competition among plants differing in such subtle adaptations to their environment determines the distribution and mix of plant species in canyons. In wet years faster-growing annuals may crowd out perennials; subsequent dry years may shift the balance back to the perennials. The abundance and distribution of herbivores and pollinators associated with these plants will also fluctuate in sympathy.

The plants and animals found in canyons may have originated in the higher altitudes of the parent mountains. Plants and animals normally found at higher elevations often occur lower down in canyons where the microclimate is cooler and wetter than surrounding areas.

Canyons may also be refugia for Ice Age plants and creatures whose nearest neighbors may occur some considerable distance away. The native palms (*Washingtonia Filifera*) of Anza-Borrego Desert State Park in California are represented by fossil remains over a much wider distribution dating from the Pleistocene. Sycamore, alder, and willow are also found in these palm canyons, displaced fifty or sixty miles from their nearest stands in the surrounding mountains. Madera Canyon in the Santa Rita Mountains of Arizona supports relict specimens of wild black cherry (*Prunus serotina*) hundreds of miles from the edge of the species' range in the central and eastern states. Stands of California black oak (*Quercus kelloggii*) grow in canyons above the town of Independence on the east slope of the Sierra Nevada, widely disjunct from the species' main distribution on the western slopes. The east slope lies in the rain shadow of the High Sierra and generally supports a Great Basin plant assemblage, although in places mixed with successful immigrants from the Sierra Nevada and Mojave Desert. The oaks in these east slope canyons are strictly riparian. It would be fascinating to know if the many specialized insects found on oaks on the west slope—leaf-mining moth larvae, gall wasps, and so on—are represented in these east slope populations. The polyphemus silk moth doesn't occur here, even though it would have many non-oak alternate hosts.

Such cases of relictualism and disjunct distributions can be explained using information gained from studies of pack rat middens and fossil pollen cores from bog and lake bottoms. During cooler and wetter ancient climates, the ranges of these now-isolated plants probably extended across much of the West as more-or-less contiguous populations or along corridors such as river systems. As the climate became warmer and drier in the last few thousand years, ranges contracted and life zones moved upslope, leaving relict stands stranded in canyons and on mountaintops.

For mobile creatures such as birds, larger mammals, and certain insects, canyons may serve as way stations for migration and dispersal. Hummingbirds, bluebirds, and hooded orioles overwinter in the palm canyons of the Anza-Borrego desert. Mule deer overwinter in southwestern canyons and disperse upslope in spring. Painted lady butterflies nectar over the winter on desert lavender in the canyons of the Mojave Desert, breed into large numbers in the spring, and often migrate en masse northward in early summer.

The greatest diversity of plants and animals is likely to be found in canyons with the most extensive and dramatic altitude gradients encompassing a wide range of plant zones. Larger mountain ranges also support greater diversity because they more effectively capture moisture and produce local rain through adiabatic cooling—the condensation of water in rising air masses.

The greatest number of endemics (species unique to the region) will probably occur in ranges isolated by some critical minimum distance from a source of colonizers—close enough to be colonized, but not so close as to be genetically homogenized by routine contact with the source population. Free of competitors, the first colonizers may adapt to new niches and evolve into new species or subspecies. These ideas can be found in the formal models of island biogeography and should apply to the "sky islands" of the American Southwest as well as to oceanic islands.

All the many factors—orientation and exposure to the sun, topography and soil types, regional climate and unique microclimates, history of colonization, and so on—interplay to give each canyon a distinct character, even compared with its

neighbor just over the next ridge. Birders, botanists, and butterfly collectors all know which canyons are favorite haunts
for their creatures, and they know as well that on every hike
the canyon will distract them from their immediate quest
and teach them something new.

※

A HIKE into Palm Canyon in the Anza-Borrego desert of
California soothes the mind at the end of the year. Even in
late December a few shrubs are in bloom—desert lavender
and the fuchsia-flowered chuparosa (*Beloperone*, the only
California member of the Acanthaceae, a group common in
the tropics, where many desert plants are thought to have
arisen)—and everywhere seeds and buds are awaiting that
one final, critical winter rain before the spring bloom in
March. The sun is warm but low in the sky at this time of
year, making for a perfect hiking temperature.

On one such winter hike I noticed how the low sun angle
highlighted the soft curves of the boulders in the creek bed,
softening an otherwise harsh terrain. The sharp, straight elements of a tracking antenna looked out of place, and I climbed
the rocky wall of the arroyo to see who was carrying these
strange metal antlers. I had an idea what they were for.

After we exchanged hellos I mumbled something about being a biologist working on an essay on canyons and asked if the two were tracking desert bighorn sheep. Esther introduced herself as a biologist from the San Diego Zoo gathering data on these threatened animals, and we chatted a bit about the perils of the bighorn's Spartan life. Because they overwinter at lower altitudes, bighorns have suffered from disease and parasites picked up from sharing water holes with domestic sheep. Until recently they were hunted to critical levels, and in the desert ranges especially, they must work hard among the boulders to find sufficient browse to feed themselves and their young. I had always thought their ability to climb steep canyon walls would protect them from predators, but Esther told me that her favorite female had just fallen victim to a cougar. We shared a few anecdotes about a professor we had by chance both taken courses from. I thanked Esther and her husband for their time and friendly conversation and we parted ways. Husband carried just enough gear to be useful, but struck a good balance by not overloading himself on the steep and rugged path they followed up a side canyon. The UHF frequency the sheep collars send to the tracking radio tends to bounce off canyon walls, and spotting the sheep requires experience and intuition in tracking the animal until you are in a direct line of sight. Such is the lot of field biologists, a dedicated but underpaid subspecies.

※

WHEN ASKED if I am ever afraid to camp and hike alone in the Sierra, I always flippantly remark that the most dangerous mountain creature is my fellow man. Away from popular campgrounds, bears are shy of people and rarely seen. I've seen perhaps three or four rattlesnakes in all my time on the east slope (much more often in the coast range and western foothills), although undoubtedly I have passed by many more, unnoticed by me and ignored by them. After a few decades of hunting bans, our cougar population has rebounded. Young male cougars trying to establish their own hunting ranges have encountered the expanding human range as people build homes in rural areas to avoid congestion and unaffordable urban housing. Domestic pets are far easier prey than the traditional mule deer. Human and cougar ecological niches now slightly overlap in these areas. This isn't true in wild, unsettled areas. In forty years of fieldwork and hiking I have never seen a cougar in the wild. Wildlife biologists reassure me that this is a testimony to the cougar's stealth, cryptic coloration, and natural avoidance of man, and not a reflection on my naturalist's skills. "If cougars don't want to be seen," they tell me, "you just won't see them!" On one collecting trip I discovered the truth of this remark.

I was camping along Leviathan Creek, in the center of the *Hyalophora* hybrid zone, in a spot where the creek had cut a not-quite-a-canyon gully in rolling pinyon country just east of Monitor Pass. Over the years the creek had meandered, rising and falling many times, cutting away at its banks. Its sandy margins were free of thick foliage. After setting out a trap line of funnel traps earlier that afternoon, I had made and eaten dinner and now was taking an evening stroll in the fading light. After a few minutes I turned around and began walking back to my campsite. Around a bend I looked down to see giant cat prints in the sand, neatly interspersed between my own.

I was fascinated rather than afraid, and slowly followed the tracks until they veered off and up into the rocks and pinyons. The big cat had tracked me for perhaps forty or fifty feet. I would like to be able to say that I had sensed something, that my hair stood on end for no perceptible reason. I had been absorbing the nature around me—keenly attentive to the bird songs, the smell of the willow, the color of the sagebrush — and was oblivious to the cougar behind me. For years I had collected, photographed, investigated, and documented nature; now it was nature's turn to judge me. And I was found wanting—not a suitable prey item—just as a mantis takes a measure of a beetle and finds it too large to capture. I remember having similar thoughts that evening, smiling and walking back to camp perhaps too casually, looking occasionally over my shoulder. I slept in the truck that night.

CHAPTER FOUR

Over the Pass

MY FIRST SEMESTER at Berkeley nearly overwhelmed me. I took too many courses, the East Bay culture was too great a diversion from classes, and the academic competition was much keener than I had experienced in high school. My little book on wild silk moth natural history may have helped me gain entrance to Berkeley, but this recognition was quickly forgotten and I was promptly swallowed up by large classes filled with voracious pre-med students. Although a zoology major, I sought solace in the company of lepidopterists at the California Academy of Sciences and in the Entomology Department at Berkeley. Jerry Powell, a new professor in the department interested in moths, showed me a few specimens of *Hyalophora gloveri* in the collection from the east slope of the Sierra Nevada. I hadn't known that *gloveri* could be found west of the Wasatch Range in Utah, but if it did occupy the east slope of the Sierra, then I knew from Sweadner's writings that it surely must hybridize with its close relative *euryalus*, which blankets the west slope and coast range mountains of the entire Pacific Coast.

There were no known hybrids in museum or university collections, nor were any known to collectors I talked to. The High Sierra peaks and ridges apparently separated the two, but could there be a low pass that allowed contact and exchange of genes? If so, I had a chance to make a valuable discovery and perhaps do research in California that would extend Sweadner's work with the same two species in the Bitterroots of the Northwest.

In my junior year I took G. Ledyard Stebbins's course in the genetics of evolution. Stebbins (not to be confused with the herpetologist Robert C. Stebbins, also of Berkeley) was a botanist and one of the founders of the "evolutionary synthesis." The seminal work for this renaissance in evolutionary biology was written by a Russian émigré, Theodosius Dobzhansky, in 1937. Dobzhansky combined laboratory and population genetics—largely from work with *Drosophila* flies—with traditional systematics to explain the genetic divergence of populations and geographical races leading to the founding of new species. In 1859 Darwin had proposed natural selection as the mechanism for the origin of adaptations and of new species, but without an understanding of the basis of heredity Darwin didn't know the source of the variation on which selection acted. The science of genetics began in 1900 with the discovery of Gregor Mendel's work. As described in the new synthesis, genetics provided the mechanism for the process of natural selection and established the continuity through heredity for the evolution over time of biological diversity.

By the 1960s genetics was a mature science with heavy emphasis on molecular biology describing the encoding and translation of genes. This new knowledge complemented work from classical genetics on the chromosomal mechanisms that recombine genes in sexual reproduction. Mathematical models described how selection acts on this pool of genetic diversity in natural populations. Stebbins had just finished a manuscript for a textbook book entitled *Processes of Organic Evolution*, and we were assigned to read and critique a chapter each week. I was an eager student, and more through zeal than superior intellect managed to tie for the highest grade in the class. The following spring I gathered up a few cocoons of *Hyalophora* and headed for the east slope with my friend and mentor Don MacNeill from the Cal Academy.

A former college football player, Don would surely shatter any shallow stereotype of a wispy butterfly collector. Don's special interest was in the small, fast-flying skippers, an enigmatic group, neither moth nor true butterfly, and at that time poorly known both taxonomically and ecologically. We soon discovered a shared love of fieldwork. On our moth trip he introduced me to the eastern Sierra Nevada with its immense vistas of sagebrush-covered slopes and massive granite formations unobstructed by the dense, sometimes claustrophobic, forests of the western slopes. The difference in plant communities on the two slopes is due to the interaction of topography and weather. The east slope is a steep escarpment on the lee side of the Sierra formation. Pacific storms batter the gradual slopes of the Sierra's western side, but the peaks and backbone crest of the mountains form a rain shadow to the east.

We found a campsite along a creek lined with coyote willow (*Salix exigua*, a *gloveri* food plant) and cooked a meal over dead sagebrush and the hard, hot-burning branches of mountain mahogany. Later, Don made "twisties"—Bisquik dough wrapped around green willow sticks, baked over the fire, and then filled with jelly. I put on a few extra layers to keep out

Hyalophora gloveri trapped along Walker River, Mono Co., Calif., just south of the hybrid zone. Variation in the shape of the hind wing eyespot shows the effect of gene flow through the hybrid zone from *H. euryalus*, which always have the elongated spot shown in the upper specimens. The kidney-shaped spot on the bottom two specimens typifies the Great Basin and Rocky Mountain *gloveri*.

the cold that penetrated the cotton sleeping bag I had borrowed from one of Don's daughters. Giving my caged female moths a final check, I warned Don that if the magic worked, I might be waking him just before dawn. As a butterfly collector, he was less than enthusiastic about this prospect.

About 4:00 AM I woke to the sound of wings beating against the screen cage. The cold predawn air at six thousand feet did not slow down the moths' biological clocks, and right on schedule male *Hyalophora* began sailing gracefully over my sleeping bag; one found the cage and crawled and fluttered in a frenzy of lustful frustration as he tried to reach the female. Shivering in my sleeping bag, I was impressed that these "cold-blooded" creatures could be so active at these temperatures—certainly it was not much more than 40 degrees F. Years later I would learn that their furry bodies actually do keep them warm by trapping the heat their flight muscles generate, which allows the moths to invade a time niche after the main period of bat activity and before the birds awake. I had to collect a number of males to get a statistical sample, so I slipped this first male and the others that followed into glassine envelopes. I shook Don from his sleep and he managed a good imitation of genuine interest.

At dawn he truly shared my excitement to see in good light

the nature of the beasts we had trapped. The Rocky Mountains populations of *gloveri* unvaryingly have small, kidney-shaped eyespots on their hind wings; the wings are rich burgundy separated by a wide white band from a speckling of salt-and-pepper scales near the wing margin. The West Coast *euryalus* have very long, comma-shaped hind wing eyespots and uniformly red wings with a narrow white band. Yet in my hands I held a moth that generally resembled a *gloveri* but had enlarged and pointed eyespots exactly intermediate in size and shape between the two "good" species, and with a mixture of red, white, and black scales just as I had seen in the artificial hybrids I had produced from cage matings! We also noticed quite a bit of variation in the size and shape of the eyespot. Don agreed with me that this might indicate extensive gene exchange—introgression—from *euryalus* into the *gloveri* populations we had just sampled. We were camped north of the town of Bridgeport along Highway 395 just north of the Sonora Pass turnoff. Could there be a pass near here, perhaps to the north where the High Sierra crest dips down, where I would find a complete transition from one species to the other, a "hybrid zone" as described in the genetics journals? It was five more years, after graduation and a stint in the Vietnam—era navy, before I was able to try to answer this question.

CHAPTER FIVE

Sibling Species
in Sagebrush Meadows

STEVE MILLER AND I renewed our earlier acquaintance through a mutual collector friend, a headmaster at an eastern boy's academy with whom we had both been corresponding. I first met Steve in 1962 when he visited my caterpillar farm while he was still in high school and I was home for the summer from college. We had not kept in touch. Steve had moved to California to work for a Quaker school in the Sierra foothills as an alternative to military service during the Vietnam War era. I had finished college and served several years in the navy, part of the time on an aircraft carrier. As therapy after these troubled times we both had found an escape in our boyhood interest in collecting and rearing moths.

We also shared a fascination for a group of day-flying silk

moths within the genus *Hemileuca*, so called because several of the species have semitransparent, black-and-white-banded wings. I had just purchased a new book on North American silk moths written by Douglas Ferguson of the U.S. National Museum in Washington, D.C., in which the author commented that *H. eglanterina* (named after Shakespeare's "eglantine rose" in *A Midsummer Night's Dream*) showed remarkable geographic variation but was nevertheless distinct from a very similar "sibling" species, *H. nuttalli.* These *Hemileuca* species were called "sheep moths" by the nineteenth-century entomologists who discovered them in sagebrush meadows where sheep were herded (anyone familiar with domestic sheep might think this moniker slighted the moths). Although they could be found together in the Rocky Mountains and Great Basin, the two species seemed never to interbreed in spite of their close resemblance in form, color, and habits. Many earlier workers, including William Jacob Holland in his *Moth Book,* had missed the subtle but consistent differences between the two and had lumped them together as the same species (see plate 8). Ferguson had worked mostly with museum specimens, and he left open many questions about their life history that a western collector could answer. Just as important, the sibling species and a closely related third species, *H. hera,* all occurred on Monitor Pass where I had been working. Here where the western border of the Great Basin meets the High Sierra I had found another chance to combine the solitude of hiking and camping with science.

Steve and I brought a reared *eglanterina* female up to Monitor Pass to use as a lure for local males. *Hemileuca* males are fast, erratic fliers, and the shrubby terrain was difficult, so bait was our only hope of capturing them. Trying to net them would result only in the ultimate parody of a mad butterfly collector. On the western slopes of the Sierra, *eglanterina* is brightly colored with pink, yellow, and orange, but in the Great Basin the fore wings are creamy white with diffuse black bands. The series of males we collected, then and later, showed that the pass is indeed an area where the two *eglanterina* forms blend together in an intergrade population. This was evidence that from the standpoint of reproductive isolation the eastern and western slope populations are the same species.

Incoming males changed their flight to a slow and deliberate fluttering as they neared the female—almost a change in mood when faced with the serious prospect of mating. This may be typical behavior for the big moths, but it normally occurs in the middle of the night and is very difficult to witness. It was fascinating to watch in full daylight as the males followed pheromone trails. Suddenly, we were startled to see a male of the other species approaching. We recognized him in flight by his white forewing and yellow hind wings, each sharply marked with distinctive black bands. Steve deftly netted him, but I insisted that we let the next *nuttalli* approach undisturbed. I wanted to take advantage of mating insects' propensity to remain oblivious to all but the most intrusive human presence and observe this interspecies attraction. Several more *nuttalli* came in and we resisted our instinct to sweep them out of the air. Unlike the *eglanterina* males, they didn't enter into the slow mode of approach, but darted back and forth and then flew away. Was this an example of reproductive isolation in the act of evolving? The two species appeared to share a basic pheromone, but the *nuttalli* males lacked the ability to search out the *eglanterina* female at close range. Over time, will selection eliminate such wasteful cross attraction with its unnecessary exposure to predators?

I thought about this problem over the winter. Steve went on to steer a new course in life and tried his hand at a music career, setting aside for a time his interest in moths. Great advances had occurred in biology, especially in biochemistry and molecular genetics, while I had been away from academia. I needed a research project suitable for a master's degree to allow me catch up in these new fields as a stepping-stone toward a Ph.D. The sagebrush *Hemileuca* fit the bill. I returned to Monitor Pass the following summer, and the next, planning to spend a few weeks camped out amid the moths while I mapped out the blend zone between the two forms of *eglanterina* and documented the imperfect isolation between the two sibling species.

I set up a camp at eight thousand feet in an aspen grove off the main road. I followed a faint track left by previous camp ers, never driving too fast or straying from the route. Still, the old gal who lived with her husband and pet golden-mantled ground squirrels in the fire lookout on the peak above my campsite scolded me. "You'll be able to see them tracks for twenty years before the plants grow back." (She was right.) I chose a Eureka tent made of canvas—large, heavy, and bulky, but still in use—and covered it with cut branches to hide it from weekend tourists. During the day I collected and photo-graphed *Hemileuca* caterpillars and in general documented their natural history. Protected by stinging spines, the little larvae form feeding clusters in the spring after hatching from overwintering egg rings. They appeared to bask in the bright sun of early summer; their black color probably raises their body temperature and speeds growth in the cool air at this altitude. Birds didn't seem to bother them, and I twice found dead ants in tufts of toxic spines, but of the mature larvae I collected in midsummer about 90 percent had been parasitized by braconid and ichneumonid wasps.

I enjoyed the accessibility of these moths. In the clear mountain air I could watch them dashing across the expanse of sagebrush meadows with an abandon not seen in flitting butterflies. The big nocturnal moths like *Hyalophora* were almost as rare as geodes, except when drawn into traps, and finding caterpillars and cocoons required hours of search time. Although rarity adds to the enjoyment of discovery, the bright abundance of the *Hemileuca* was enchanting. Sometimes I even found them resting in late afternoon, their boldly patterned wings tented over their bodies (see plates 9, 10, and 11). If touched, a resting moth would drop to the ground, raise its wings over its back, and curl its abdomen downward, exposing bright yellow and black rings. The moths advertise the rings by pulsing the abdomen in what most biologists have interpreted as wasp-mimicking behavior. Other *Hemileuca* species similarly display red, black, or other signal colors but don't closely resemble wasps. My guess is that the

PLATES 1-4. (1) Mature (fifth instar) larva of *Hyalophora gloveri*, Mono Co., Calif. The wartlike scoli, or tubercles, of this species are larger and bear more spines than those of *H. euryalus*. (2) Fourth instar larva of *H. gloveri*, Mono Co., Calif. The red dorsal and blue lateral scoli are obscured with black pigment in many inland populations, but rarely so along the eastern slopes of the Sierra Nevada, probably due to gene introgression from the hybrid zone with *H. euryalus*. (3) The mature larva of *H. euryalus* differs from that of *H. gloveri* in having smaller scoli with fewer spines. (4) Fourth instar larva of *H. euryalus*. The dorsal scoli are always yellow, never red or black as in *H. gloveri*. These scoli and the blue scoli on the sides are usually smaller than those of *H. gloveri*. Larvae in the hybrid zone between the two species often have orange dorsal scoli, a mixture of the two parental species' colors. All photographs by the author.

(1)

(2)

(3)

(4)

PLATE 5. *Eupackardia calleta* larva. The
gaudy color and pattern suggest warning
coloration, as does the blood chemistry.
Photograph by Kirby L. Wolfe.

PLATE 6. *Eupackardia calleta* caterpillar feeding on ocotillo. Madera Canyon, Santa Rita Mountains, south of Tucson, Ariz. At a distance, the coloration of these larvae renders them somewhat cryptic against the plant background. Photograph by the author.

PLATE 7. The adult *Eupackardia calleta* may be a mimic of the distasteful pipevine swallowtail. Photograph by William Mooney.

PLATE 8. Sibling species of *Hemileuca* moths. Photograph by the author.

Left, top to bottom: Hemileuca eglanterina. On Monitor Pass (Alpine and Mono Cos., Calif.) the light east slope form (*top*) intergrades into the yellow/pink/orange form (*bottom*) found on the Sierra Nevada west slope.

Right, top two specimens: Hemileuca hera (female above, male below; Monitor Pass, Mono Co., Calif.) is distinct in its pheromones and mating behavior, its white and black coloration, and its larval host, *Artemisia* (sagebrush). *Third and fourth from top: Hemileuca nuttalli* from Monitor Pass. At one time *nuttalli* was listed as a subspecies of *eglanterina,* with which it shares larval host plants. Subtle differences in pheromones and mating behavior isolate the two sibling species where they co-occur. *Bottom:* East Humboldt Range, Elko Co., Nev. This unusually large form from the interior mountains of Nevada resembles *Hemileuca eglanterina* and is attracted to *eglanterina* females from California, but may prove to be a distinct species.

PLATE 9. Resting adult of *Hemileuca hera*. Photograph by the author.

PLATE 10. *Hemileuca eglanterina*, the reddish orange form found on the western slope of the Sierra Nevada. Photograph by Kirby L. Wolfe.

PLATE 11. A mating pair of *Hemileuca nuttalli*. Photograph by Arthur M. Shapiro.

(1)

(2)

PLATE 12. Variation in wing pattern of *Hyalophora* moths in the hybrid zone, Monitor Pass, Mono and Alpine Cos., Calif. (1) Wild male *H. gloveri* (*right*, Ruby Mountains, Elko Co., Nev.) mating with a tethered bred female *H. euryalus* (*left*, Monterey Co., Calif.); note different hind wing eyespot shapes. Female hybrid offspring from such pairings of

(3)

(4)

geographically distant parents are sterile; Monitor Pass, California, wild hybrid females are fertile. (2), (3), (4). Wild-collected males from the Monitor Pass hybrid zone showing a range of variation that is generally intermediate between the patterns of the two parental species. (3) is an unusual phenotype with the reddish color of *euryalus* but small hind wing eyespots like those of *gloveri*. All photographs by the author.

(top) PLATE 13. The West Coast species, *Hyalophora euryalus* (Nevada Co., Calif.), is uniformly reddish with narrow white lines and elongated hind wing eyespots.

(bottom) PLATE 14. The Great Basin and Rocky Mountain species, *Hyalophora gloveri* (White Mountains, Inyo Co., Calif.), is a burgundy wine red with wide white bands and black and white scales beyond these bands. The hind wing eyespot is always a blunt oval. This eyespot difference can be measured and used as an index of hybridization between *H. euryalus* and *H. gloveri*. Both photographs by the author.

Hemileuca species as a group are bitter tasting, a very common trait in warningly colored Lepidoptera, but I have not personally taste-tested this or set up experiments to confirm the idea.

My friend Lincoln Brower and his wife, Jane VanZandt, gained fame by performing just such an experiment, a landmark in evolutionary ecology. They reared nestling blue jays as naïve predators, feeding them palatable viceroy butterflies, a supposed mimic of the poisonous monarch. The birds eagerly accepted the viceroys and learned to recognize them by their color and pattern. When they were then offered monarchs, the jays at first could not discriminate them from viceroys. Each time they attacked a monarch they quickly spat it out and retched in response to the cardiac glycosides these butterflies sequester from milkweed during the larval stage. (Revealing his wry humor, Brower quantified glycoside levels in standard "emetic units.") Still reeling from the experiment, the wretched birds subsequently refused to feed on viceroy adults, presumably solely on the basis of their visual resemblance to monarchs. More than a century after Henry Walter Bates proposed the idea of mimicry, the Browers and their students linked together plant biochemistry and predation to explain the evolution of warning coloration in the monarch model and of convergent patterns on the wings of the viceroy mimic. The color and behavior of the *Hemileuca* species should tempt someone to repeat this kind of study; merely arranging the attractive moths in a specimen case doesn't tell their story in nature.

In the evenings I would enjoy the stillness and the quiet songs of the few sage sparrows who continued to call past their assigned day shift. A slow evening walk would often treat me to a flock of sage hens (the local name—serious birders call them sage grouse) or a curious coyote that would regard me for a moment before returning to its mouse hunt. At night I would turn on my little transistor radio and listen to distant stations as the night sky—undisturbed by the sun's ionizing effect—skipped radio waves off the ionosphere. How strange to hear of Agnew's resignation and Nixon's growing Watergate woes and, oddly, to feel as oblivious to it all as my mule deer companions.

Compared with my own species, the lives of even the caterpillars were more harmonious. Next year's crop of eggs, laid by the few surviving adults, would surely balance out the parasites' toll. This can be a dynamic and even unstable balance. One year, perhaps following a bad year for parasites, the *Hemileuca* larvae were extraordinarily abundant on one slope below the lookout tower, and almost every snowberry was partially defoliated by larvae of both *nuttalli* and *eglanterina*. A week later a viral disease appeared and nearly wiped out this entire local population. The flux in numbers of larvae, pupae, and moths, and of their parasites, probably had a ripple effect on other organisms in this community. Did the defoliated shrubs manage to produce seeds? Did the loss of parasite larvae along with their stricken hosts affect the populations of other Lepidoptera normally attacked by these same parasites?

By simply camping out and doing basic fieldwork I could see firsthand how life history adaptations are integrated into a survival strategy. A species is a structural beam in the cathedral of complexity that is a biotic community. These beams interlock through predation, competition, herbivory, and other interactions. The failure of a beam weakens the structure; the fate of one species affects other plants and animals in fascinating and unpredictable ways. The work involved in observing, teasing apart, and experimenting with a life history is worth the considerable time and effort needed to understand the architecture of community life.

The moths eclosed in late summer, and my stock of reared females emerged in synchrony. With baited traps I captured hundreds of *eglanterina* and with a felt pen gave each a unique number coded as dots at specific positions on the wings. The marked males I recovered told me how long the average male lived (about five days) and how far he traveled (an average of about one mile). I showed that the pink, yellow, and orange phase on the western slopes did in fact gradually blend into the light-colored form in the sagebrush meadows of Monitor Pass. Crosses between these and other "races" of *eglanterina* never uncovered any sterility or other reproductive incompatibility that would suggest they are more than subspecies. I guessed that the lighter coloring in the sagebrush country helps in both camouflage and temperature regulation, but admitted in print that field observations alone were insufficient proof. My data did show that the light color form was more common in plant communities with sagebrush as the dominant cover, and, as expected, that the percentage return of marked-and-released light-colored moths was highest in these areas. The pinkish form was more common in mixed shrub communities, where it also had a higher rate of return. Apparently, the association of wing color and plant background was somehow correlated with survival, probably on the basis of crypsis as a foil to bird predation. (A few moths of both color forms were recaptured with fresh beak marks, but the numbers were too low to analyze.) This hypothesis would be hard to prove even with a team of researchers collecting data over many years.

※

INDUSTRIAL MELANISM IN MOTHS, long cited in biology texts as a lesson in natural selection, should be—for this discussion—the most relevant and compelling example of genetic adaptation to environmental features. Recently, this classic story has become controversial. Its complexity, its importance to science, and its relevance to society's use and misuse of scientific concepts are quite beyond the scope of this work, but the subject deserves at least an introduction.

Once rare in England, a melanic morph of the normally light-colored peppered moth (*Biston betularia*) was seen to increase in frequency near areas of industrial pollution, where lichens became scarce. In unpolluted areas the light-colored form is assumed to be cryptic on lichen-covered tree trunks because of its color and pattern. Historical collections, and subsequent research by H. B. D. Kettlewell, clearly established the correlation between the rise of the dark morph and the onset of the Industrial Revolution. With the imposition of pollution controls, the relative frequency of the two

morphs shifted again, with the reappearance of the light phenotype coinciding with the recovery of lichens. Kettlewell
conducted mark-release-recapture studies with reared animals to prove that bird predation on resting moths was the
agent of selection favoring the dark morph on darkened tree
trunks and the light form on lichens. Most biology texts show
these morphs at rest on the appropriate substrate.

Kettlewell's research methods and conclusions have been
criticized as less than rigorous by today's standards. In some
cases chilled or dead specimens were posed in unrealistical-
ly high numbers as potential prey, and we now know that
moths may not typically rest during the day on tree trunks.
Nevertheless, the correlation in time and space between the
effects of pollution and the degree of melanism in the peppered moth is an indisputable fact demanding an explanation within the Darwinian paradigm of natural selection.
The ecological genetic basis of industrial melanism in these
moths is more complex than originally thought. Differential
predation on adult morphs likely plays a key role in maintaining the geographic pattern of melanism, although there
is some evidence that the *larvae* of melanic moths have a
physiological advantage in certain environments.

This tale of natural selection remains a fascinating example of "evolution in action," in spite of the hyperbole from creationists exploiting criticism of the original work. Criticism, replication of experiment and observation, and reevaluation of past work are the strengths of science, not a sign of weakness; they are a maturing process in scientific research. The peppered moth story is only one tale in the development of the School of Ecological Genetics at Oxford University established by the elitist, autocratic, and delightfully eccentric E. B. Ford. Readers interested in the history of this research and the colorful characters behind it should consult *Of Moths and Men* by Judith Hooper (Norton, 2002).

IN PLANNING further research with the *Hemileuca* moths, I knew the basis of reproductive isolation among the species would be easier to investigate than the adaptive basis of the wing color variation. With the help of my friend (and future coauthor) Paul Tuskes from UC Davis, I set out widely spaced traps, each baited with one of the three species. Wild males of all three forms were then presented with a taxonomic choice, and by trapping them and observing their behavior we could make much more definite conclusions about reproductive isolation in the group.

Paul and I found that the *eglanterina* males responded only to their own females, and that most were trapped between 10:00 AM and noon. In the wild, most females would be mated by midday, but caged *eglanterina* females—unable to mate—continued "calling" past this time and thus drew in a few *nuttalli* males. In nature, only the odd unmated female would be at risk of mating with the wrong species. Most of these *nuttalli* males could not find the caged *eglanterina* female, but a few did; about 15 percent of an afternoon's catch would be composed of the wrong species. The interspecific attraction was not symmetrical. Caged *nuttalli* females released pheromone only from noon on, and never attracted *eglanterina* males. Females of the third species, *H. hera*, attracted only their own species, and *hera* males never entered traps baited with the other species. Ecologically *hera* is quite different as well. The larvae eat only the pungent, aromatic leaves of sagebrush (a North American relative of the wormwood from which absinthe is extracted), one of very few insects to do so.

When I cross-mated *eglanterina* and *nuttalli* in the lab, the females laid only a few ova, and most of these did not hatch. The hybrid caterpillars died in a few days. In spite of their wing pattern similarity and their nearly identical life histories, these are clearly distinct species. In the wild, interbreeding between *nuttalli* and *eglanterina* is prevented by a sequence of barriers, none entirely effective in itself: time of attraction, an imperfect and asymmetrical behavioral response to the other species' pheromone (shown twenty years later by my friend Steve McElfresh to be based on the structural chemistry of the molecules), and genetic differences that disrupt embryo development. In nature, the larvae of the two can be found side by side on the same snowberry bush, yet they almost never hybridize. Of about seven hundred caterpillars I collected over a decade, only one produced a hybrid adult. Not perfect isolation, but good enough to let the two species continue to evolve independently. In this respect the *Hemileuca* are very different from the *Hyalophora*, which are distinct in color and markings but weakly isolated reproductively. The nature of species has to be studied in nature and cannot be found in specimen drawers, no matter how enchanting the variation in color and pattern.

CHAPTER SIX

Hybrid Zones
and Rattlesnake Cages

WHEN I RETURNED from my tour of duty in the navy, I began planning a program of moth trapping to track down the *Hyalophora* hybrid zone I knew must exist near where Don MacNeill and I had collected five years earlier. I fashioned a trap consisting of a metal funnel mounted atop a screen cylinder. As bait I set a small cage holding an unmated female over the mouth of the funnel. Males would find the female and in their frenzy to mate eventually slide down the funnel. The bait female would continue to call in males until dawn. By setting out a line of traps I could census a large area, including transects up mountain slopes through various plant zones and over passes across the Sierra Nevada. I could then examine the wing characters—the phenotype—of the captured males and determine the limits of the ranges of *Hyalophora gloveri* and *H. euryalus* and the location of the predicted hybrid zone where they overlapped.

Near the town of Markleeville I collected moths largely resembling *euryalus*, but also a few with hybrid characters. The road over Monitor Pass begins at five thousand feet along the Carson River near Markleeville, climbs a steep canyon lined at its base with cottonwoods, and crests an armlike extension of the Sierra. The entire region is in the rain shadow of the Sierra Nevada and is therefore mostly covered with a sagebrush scrub community with scattered Jeffrey pine, the east slope twin to ponderosa pine. On slopes near the summit the trees themselves are a hybrid blend of Jeffrey pine mixed with white fir and lodgepole pine more typical of western slopes. Near the summit, at about eight thousand feet, aspen groves dominate. The eastern descent opens to a grand vista of the Sweetwater Mountains to the east and continues down toward Topaz Lake and Highway 395 through stands of pinyon pine. The scenery is spectacular any time of year, but perhaps especially so in the fall when the aspen and rabbit brush turn complementary shades of yellow.

For me, Monitor Pass is literally like no other place in the world because here I finally found the zone where all the

Hyalophora are hybrids, blending into the *gloveri* phenotype to the south and east, and into pure *euryalus* to the west near Lake Tahoe. In one trap I collected about two dozen moths, no two alike, exhibiting extraordinary variation. I was sure this was due to extensive hybridization and genetic recombination within the population. Very few of the adults could be classified unequivocally as either species. What could this population of hybrids tell me about the nature of genetic differences between closely related species, and about the process of speciation itself? I spread a series of specimens, and with my master's degree in hand began looking for a graduate school where I could find answers to these questions.

Perhaps prospective graduate students at Ivy League schools dress in suit and tie to meet and talk with professors, hoping to impress with their knowledge of the professor's field and their proposals for original work. And in the stiff and contrived formality of academia the professor indulgently nods and poses carefully worded questions to evaluate the potential student. Perhaps this ritual also occurs at Stanford, but

FACING PAGE:

The author in 1971 examining a catch of *Hyalophora* moths trapped along the Walker River (Mono Co., Calif.) south of Monitor Pass. This type of funnel trap allowed a systematic sampling along a transect over Monitor Pass.

that was not my experience at the University of California at Davis! I had made an appointment, at Jerry Powell's suggestion, to meet a new professor in the Zoology Department who had already established a reputation for intense energy and original insights in current research in ecology and evolution. And he was a lepidopterist. I had dressed in garb appropriate for such a meeting at UC Davis—slacks and a short-sleeved shirt. Under my arm was a glass-covered specimen case with several of the wild hybrids I had collected at Monitor Pass.

Davis is in the Sacramento Valley, and because the entire area is flat, nearly everyone rides a bicycle on campus. Invariably they ride too fast. As I walked toward an entrance to campus, blocked to vehicles by steel posts set in the ground, a student came rushing at me, swerved to avoid the posts, and collided with me as I stood there in amazement, thinking that surely he would slow down and ride around me. I managed to cushion the impact on the specimen case, and the moths were intact, but when I stood up and looked down I saw that I was badly cut and bleeding. Satisfied that the homicidal cyclist's wheel spokes were already sufficiently bent, I found the zoology building and went to the men's room to wash up as best I could. Except for the wounds, I didn't look much more disheveled than most of the students. As I entered the lab I saw a figure in the professor's chair, feet up on the desk, wearing black-and-white Keds whose like I hadn't seen since ninth grade. His head sported a beard and long hair project- ing outward at random angles. Assuming he was a graduate student, I asked, "Can you tell me where Professor Shapiro is?" "I'm Art Shapiro," he answered, reaching for a band-aid. "What happened to you?"

With that novel introduction there was no need to break the ice, and Art and I quickly became engrossed in learning about each other's work. He was right on top of all the lat- est hybrid zone theory and eagerly encouraged me to apply because he thought my Monitor Pass results would make a good thesis topic. I soon discovered that he expected his Ph.D. candidates to bring well-thought-out ideas for original work, and that if you didn't pursue and defend your own ideas, he would quickly lead the conversation into intense lectures on his latest work with pierid butterflies. That suited me fine since in either situation I knew I could learn a lot quickly. We remain close friends and still share ideas.

In the 1950s and 1960s, hybrid zones were looked upon as evidence that speciation is a gradual process. In this view, spe- cies are the end product of genetic changes that occurred as geographical races adapted to different and changing environments. Such subspecies might subtly differ in appearance or in natural history adaptations and yet be considered members of a single species. The test for species status was whether races would freely interbreed where their ranges overlapped or when brought together in the laboratory. Natural history guides for birds and butterflies are filled with examples of subspecies that are distinct in certain regions but blend together where their ranges meet.

As races continue to evolve, they eventually become so different that their hybrid offspring are somehow unfit—weak, sterile, or maladapted to their environment. At this point we would be justified in calling them separate species. But making such decisions is difficult if the taxonomist is working with widely separated races that do not meet in nature and cannot easily be experimentally hybridized. Indeed, species pairs that successfully interbreed in captivity may not elect to mate in the wild. Taxonomic decisions are not usually based on experimental hybridization; insects are an exception in this regard, especially fruit flies (*Drosophila*) and some butterflies and moths. For geographically isolated forms, taxonomists up to the 1980s more often did comparative studies of morphology—color, pattern, and structure—and made their best guess on the basis of experience whether or not two taxa were "good" species. *Homo sapiens* is a special case; we have performed such "experimental" interbreeding countless times—enough to establish that our racial divisions are trivial in spite of superficial differences.

At one time hybrid zones were thought to be formed when two populations in the final stage of speciation came together; genetic differences would produce unfit hybrids, yet the two forms would still be so similar in mate recognition and mating behavior that they would freely interbreed. This was the view of Charles Remington of Yale University, founder of the Lepidopterists' Society, who was influenced by his earlier acquaintance with Sweadner in promoting the study of hybrid zones as an opportunity to view speciation in progress. Remington predicted that hybrid zones would be short-lived and eliminated as selection favored the evolution of antihybridization barriers, the final stage of speciation in his model. In 1968 Remington published a paper on "suture zones," which he defined as regions where pairs of closely related species, of a variety of taxonomic groups, independently met and hybridized following a phase of range expansion at the end of the Ice Age. Remington documented several such zones in North America and predicted that hybridization would be found in others he designated. The fact that species pairs of such unrelated groups as birds, mammals, and butterflies all met in such areas meant that some aspect of the topography brought them together and promoted hybridization. In some cases this was true because the region lay between refugia; other zones represented a breakdown of a natural barrier, such as a low mountain pass (the case in the Sierra Nevada *Hyalophora* hybrid zone). Remington's papers helped promote a period of intense hybrid zone research beginning in the 1970s.

As I will discuss below, we now believe that complete reproductive isolation does not necessarily accompany the overall genetic divergence that occurs during speciation. Various parts of the genome—genes controlling morphology, physiology, and reproduction—evolve at different rates. Hybridization can occur in nature between two quite differentiated species, and the resulting hybrid zones can be stable over long time spans without the evolution of reproductive isolation.

Many hybrid zones occur as narrow bands along the margin of range overlap between the two interbreeding forms, with a distinct boundary on each side where the appearance of the animals changes abruptly into that of the parent species. These distinct zones are different from the blend zones of gradual intergradation from one subspecies into another. What factors maintain these distinct boundaries? Many zones occur in areas thought to have been reinvaded as natural ranges expanded at the end of the Ice Age some eight to ten thousand years ago. If so, why are these narrow hybrid zones so stable? Shouldn't the two species either fuse into one or evolve mechanisms to avoid producing unfit hybrid offspring? Evolutionary biologists see hybrid zones as natural laboratories, because finding answers to these questions could help to elucidate the genetic and ecological differences between closely related species.

The *Hyalophora* moths were in many ways ideal for a hybrid zone study because they are easy to collect and readily mate in the lab. As members of the Saturniidae, they do not feed as adults and will mate and lay eggs in simple cages with little special care. I knew I could make experimental crosses and measure the fertility of eggs and the fecundity— the number of eggs that developed—of the resulting hybrid females. I could precisely quantify (biologists love hard data and sneer at anecdotal observations) the reproductive fitness of both experimental and wild individuals using stock from the hybrid zone. If I could succeed in this work, it would be the first really comprehensive empirical study of the genetic processes occurring in a hybrid zone. In Art Shapiro's words, I could "find out at last what makes hybrid zones tick."

I also planned to rear caterpillars in cages at sites along a transect through the hybrid zone. One theory explaining what maintains boundaries on hybrid zones held that hybrids are ecologically adapted only to transitional areas—ecotones—where one plant community changes into another. Outside these intermediate areas only one or the other parent species is ecologically successful. Some biologists believed that the hybrids might actually be better adapted to ecotones than the parent forms. This very local ecological superiority would explain the stability of the hybrid zone.

To test this model I could rear three replicate lots—the two pure species and experimental hybrids—and measure the percentage hatch, survival, and growth rate of the caterpillars on different plants to see if either regional climate or plant species were agents of natural selection operating in the hybrid zone. I devised a collapsible wire mesh and screen cage I could carry into the "field" and set up over selected bushes. My fieldwork involved climbing up and down steep, rocky slopes at altitudes up to eight thousand feet, but I loved being outdoors and didn't mind the hard work when I could end the day in a cabin or campsite with a cold beer and a good meal. The breeding experiments would reveal if hybrids were reproductively unfit in terms of sterility or viability.

The other accepted model of hybrid zones held that sterility or other physiological unfitness confines hybrids to narrow zones. In this "tension zone" model, the width of the zone is determined by an equilibrium between gene flow from the parent populations (migrants into the hybrid zone that interbreed with the other species), which would tend to widen the zone, and selection against unfit hybrids, which would tend to narrow the zone. If one sex among hybrids was nearly or fully fertile, then backcrossing would produce a wide range of genetic variation among individuals in the zone, rather than completely sterile hybrid individuals, each with an equal contribution of genes from the two parent species but with no reproductive potential. In this latter case, the zone would collapse into a very narrow band where both parental forms would occur together, along with occasional hybrid individuals.

By the early 1980s population geneticists using powerful computers had simulated these complex models of hybrid zone genetics and produced a series of stimulating articles. In the simplest models, the theoreticians saw hybrid zones as composed of a series of clines, slopes graphically depicting gene frequency plotted against distance. Like installing incompatible programs into a computer, genes from one species that control some highly adaptive trait, such as reproductive fitness, might not function properly against the mixed genetic background of hybrids or that of the opposite species. Hybrids possessing these incompatible gene combinations would leave few or no offspring, and selection would then produce a steep cline for the frequency of this gene plotted against distance across the zone. Other genes that might favor hybrids, especially in intermediate environments, would tend to spread and be seen as smoother clines, as would genes that were neutral in effect regardless of the genetic background of the individual carrying them.

Opposing the effect of selection would be the dispersal ability of the animals, which would tend to widen clines through migration and interbreeding. Steep clines would be the result of either strong selection or weak gene flow. Wider clines would result from weak selection and high dispersal ability. The hybrid zone could then be depicted as a summation of the clinal variation in genes regulating key traits, such as fertility, development of the embryo, viability, and growth rate of life history stages, all of which would be subject to intense selection in the hybrid zone. I was not a good enough mathematician to help formulate these theoretical models, but I did think I had a chance to contribute experimental data that would evaluate the validity of various models in a real hybrid zone.

Years later, in a review of my published thesis work, Larry Gall, a lepidopterist at Yale's Peabody Museum, remarked that it was "refreshing" to read my candid discussion of problems and setbacks in my fieldwork. He was being kind. What really happened was that I underestimated the determination of our little friends the deer mice (*Peromyscus*) to gnaw, chew, and dig into my cages. I think they were initially attracted by the crop of seeds on the bitterbrush (*Purshia*) bushes I chose as food plants, but once inside they happily dined on my caterpillars.

Human disturbance was never a problem. I have noticed over the years that most visitors to the Sierra are car-bound and will not wander more than a few yards off the road. A few of my cages were visible from one of the pull-offs I used as a research site, even though I covered the tops of the cages with branches. On one visit a state road maintenance truck had pulled over, and as the driver and I talked I volunteered a brief explanation of the cages, which I thought he might have noticed. "Well, that's damned innerestin'!" he said. "When I seen these people looking at them one time, I just told them they had rattlesnakes in 'em and they sure didn't want to mess with 'em after that."

One summer of rearing coincided with one of California's periodic droughts. In some of my cages, the leaves were dry

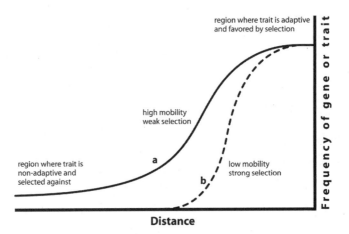

region where trait is adaptive
and favored by selection

high mobility
weak selection

region where trait is
non-adaptive and
selected against

a

low mobility
strong selection

b

Frequency of gene or trait

Distance

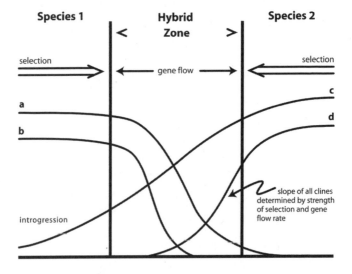

Species 1

Hybrid
Zone

Species 2

selection

< >

gene flow

selection

c

a

d

b

slope of all clines
determined by strength
of selection and gene
flow rate

introgression

and falling off the bitterbrush by August. But by conduct-
ing an extra year's work I was finally able to collect enough
data to analyze and write up my results. (Several fellow
fieldworkers in the same situation referred to ourselves as
"gradual students.")

I measured the wing patterns of hundreds of males I
collected in traps baited with virgin female moths and sub-

FACING PAGE:

Top: Genetic variation within species is partly an adaptive response to the spatial
complexity of the environment. Both biotic and nonliving factors may vary gradually
over distance. A gene variant (allele) may be adaptive in one locale but nonadaptive
in another, imposing a cline of gene frequency versus distance on intervening populations. Gene exchange among populations smoothes out this variation; weak selection
and high mobility broaden the cline (**A**), while strong selection and weak gene flow
make it steeper (**B**).

Bottom: An equilibrium model of a hybrid zone. Hybrid zones can be depicted by a
summation of clines for different traits or their underlying genes. Here, gene markers
A and **B** characterize species 1; **C** and **D** characterize species 2. Interspecific differences
in the genes controlling mating, fertilization, and embryo development may cause
incompatibility in their hybrids. Clines for such genes (**D**) will be quite abrupt across
hybrid zones. Differences in other traits may be obvious to the observer but of little
or no adaptive significance, varying as gentle clines representing introgression across
the hybrid zone into the range of the other species (marker **C**). The width and genetic
structure of hybrid zones are thought to be determined by an equilibrium between
the opposing effects of selection and gene flow. Gross morphology, enzyme variation
measured by electrophoresis, and DNA sequence markers may not vary geographically
in a concordant manner, making the boundaries of the hybrid zone somewhat
arbitrary. Studies of hybrid zones help us understand genetic changes occurring
during speciation.

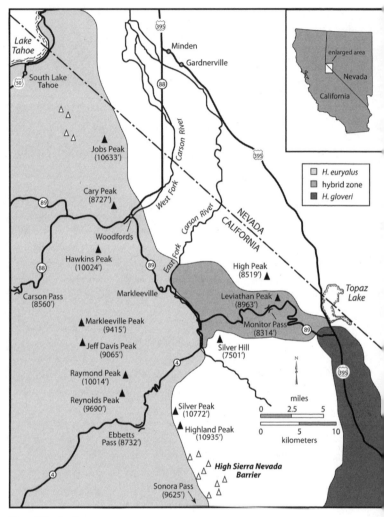

Map of Monitor Pass

jected the data to a computer analysis. In this way I established the extent of variation due to hybridization and its geographic distribution. The reddish Sierran species with the long hind wing eyespots (*Hyalophora euryalus*) occurs in pure form near Lake Tahoe. To the south, Carson Pass and Ebbetts Pass are just low enough to allow populations of *euryalus* to spill over to the east and follow the Carson River and Silver Creek drainages toward the town of Markleeville in Alpine County. Here, twenty miles southeast of Lake Tahoe, the wing patterns told me that this was the western edge of the hybrid zone. From south of Ebbetts Pass the entire Sierra crest is too high to allow *Hyalophora* to breed and so isolates the two species. Monitor Pass thus forms a rather narrow link between *euryalus* and *gloveri* and supports the hybrid zone, with few adults showing the phenotype of either parent species. There was a general trend of intergradation between *euryalus*-like moths to the west and more *gloveri*-like (the Great Basin species) moths to the east. But the variation greatly exceeded that seen in lab hybrids, suggesting to me that extensive backcrossing and genetic recombination were occurring (see plates 12, 13, 14). This in turn meant that at least one sex was not sterile within the hybrid population.

Western slope at entrance to Monitor Pass, 5,500 feet, near Markleeville (Alpine Co., Calif.), the western limit of the hybrid zone. *Hyalophora* host plants such as choke-cherry (in bloom in foreground) are largely confined to a riparian community along the Carson River. In a rain shadow of the Sierra Nevada range, the arid slopes in the background are covered with pinyon pine and Jeffrey pine.

When a *gloveri* from the Rocky Mountains is mated in the lab with a *euryalus* from California, the resulting female hybrids are barren—they appear normal in all other ways but lack eggs. Male hybrids are fertile and can successfully mate with either parent species. I was surprised to find that in the population of wild hybrids on Monitor Pass, females are fecund and hatch from their cocoons with a full complement of eggs. The hybrid zone was probably formed some eight

Sagebrush meadow at 8,000 feet near the summit of Monitor Pass, with scattered Sierra juniper, ponderosa pine, and bitterbrush. This pass is just low enough to allow *Hyalophora* to breed, thus maintaining the hybrid zone.

thousand to ten thousand years ago as the climate warmed and populations of *gloveri* expanded their Great Basin range, spreading west to the eastern slopes of the Sierra Nevada. As the many glaciers and snowfields melted, populations of *euryalus* in turn crossed over newly opened passes and met their Great Basin relatives, forming a hybrid population in the vicinity of Monitor Pass. Over the millennia of inter-breeding, selection for compatible gene combinations has

Eastern slopes of Monitor Pass, at the center of the *Hyalophora* hybrid zone, looking east toward the Sweetwater Mountains in the distance, which define the eastern limit of the hybrid zone. The Great Basin desert beyond this point is uninhabitable for *Hyalophora*. *Hyalophora* host plants such as chokecherry, bitter cherry, and antelope bitterbrush are scattered throughout this pinyon-juniper woodland.

apparently restored reproductive fitness to the hybrids. In this sense and in this one place the evolutionary process of speciation has been reversed! For all the obvious but superficial differences that taxonomists had used to distinguish the life cycle stages of *euryalus* and *gloveri*, apparently only a few key genes controlling egg development (öogenesis) truly define the evolutionary split of these two species.

This result is a general confirmation of the tension zone model of hybrid zones, but with a new wrinkle. Instead of a population of hybrids with reduced fitness, replenished every year by gene input from the bordering parental populations, the hybrid zone is self-sustaining. More exciting, I found by a series of careful experimental matings that females from a local region *within* the hybrid zone were most fertile with males from their own local population. My conclusion was that the complex topography of the region, with steep slopes and local arid regions of few host plants, acts as a partial barrier and retards the influx of parental genes from outside the zone. Protected from genetic swamping, the local optimum hybrid gene combinations—the fruit of natural selection—remain intact. A colleague from England who studies hybrid zones in Alpine crickets found a similar situation that he referred to as "local amelioration of hybrid dysfunction," a counterpart to my "regional optimization of genetic compatibility." Our findings also help to explain the stability of such hybrid zones dating back to the end of the Ice Age.

CHAPTER SEVEN

Retracing Sweadner's Steps

WITH THE PUBLICATION of the Monitor Pass *Hyalopho-
ra* hybrid zone work I felt the satisfaction of telling a story of
evolution and speciation based on an original discovery and
hard work. Of course, an honest self-appraisal in science is
an admission that we have succeeded only in revealing more
questions, certainly in such complex natural phenomena as
hybrid zones. How had selection reconstituted the hybrid genome to regain fertility in the females? Did one parent species
contribute more to this process than the other? In other words,
were the genes controlling fertility essentially all contributed
by either *gloveri* or *euryalus*? If genes controlling egg development (a trait seemingly isolated from the external environment) were really the "speciation" genes in *Hyalophora*,

why should they have come to differ in such closely related forms? At that time, in the mid-1980s, the technology of DNA sequencing had not been fully automated and commercialized, and such analyses were still quite expensive. The answers to my questions would have to wait (and are only now being addressed). This gave me an opportunity to retrace old steps and revisit a boyhood fascination.

The original inspiration for my research, Sweadner's classic study of hybridization in the Bitterroot Mountains of Idaho and Montana, still beckoned to me in many ways. I was now equipped with personal and practical experience in researching hybrid zones and had available in the literature a body of knowledge on the genetics of hybrid zones and species formation, which had become topics of intense research in the 1980s. I knew that the Bitterroots problem would not be a repeat of the Sierra Nevada work. The zone of intergradation was much wider, the moths looked different, and the topography was certainly not the same. The realms of the Pacific Northwest, Great Basin, and Rocky Mountains all merge in the region of the Bitterroots, which form the border between Idaho and Montana. I was anxious to begin working on a new problem and to explore and experience the natural history of this part of the country. It would be an adventure. Finally, the story of Sweadner the person was compelling—of his solitary trek over crude mountain roads in a Model A truck during the harsh Depression years that eventually led to a key paper in evolutionary biology. I wanted to publish some kind of biography of Sweadner, but first I had to retrace his steps.

Over the years I had made a few trips to the Bitterroots, but without much success. I had collected a few moths, but no females from which to rear experimental broods. No one, including Sweadner, had described the life stages, and hybrid broods between Bitterroots males and eastern *cecropia* females seemed to indicate that the early stages in the Bitterroots population were quite distinctive. Part of the problem was the weather. The weather in June, when the moths fly, is broken up by cold rainstorms from the Pacific Northwest. The Bitterroots were a long way from my home, and successful collecting would mean staying in the field long enough to wait out rainy weather.

It was 1989 by the time I was able to muster enough time and livestock to make the trip worthwhile. I brought an ultraviolet black light to try to collect a wild female from which I could get eggs. Sweadner had followed a route from Helena, Montana, to Coeur d'Alene, Idaho. This route is now a four-lane divided highway, so setting out funnel traps was not always practical. For part of my transect over the Bitter-roots' crest I chose the Lolo Pass Highway and scouted out the terrain near Lolo Hot Springs. The original hot springs was a favorite summer recreation spot during Sweadner's time and earlier. The old stone lodge displayed photographs of vacationers surrounded by wagons, buggies, and canvas tents. In the early 1980s the lodge had been operated by a middle-aged man with a gray beard and ponytail, kept company by a giant sleeping Saint Bernard and a stuffed moose head, all three with similar droopy expressions. Small cabins surrounded an indoor, swimsuit-optional, hot pool. By 1989, sadly, the lodge had been taken over by a Christian funda-mentalist group that had erected a high pine-wood fence to keep out the public, especially evolutionary biologists. Long gone were the bar and gambling rooms made famous in the book and movie *A River Runs through It.*

I turned up a logging road near the hot springs after set-ting out a trap line of my funnel traps, each baited with a virgin female. After a quick meal I made a small fire, set up the black light, and decided to turn in early because the mountain air turns quickly cold at this altitude and latitude. I slept fitfully and just before midnight crawled out of my sleeping bag to investigate a rustling sound. In the beam of my flashlight was a tiny shrew dashing about in search of insects and worms. These little insectivores (they aren't rodents) probably have the highest metabolic rate of all mammals and need to eat more than their body weight every day to stay alive. The shrew was oblivious to my light, and I followed it until it disappeared in leaves and brambles. As I returned to my campsite I checked the black light. There on the sheet, just at ground level, was a female *Hyalophora*, the critical find I needed to begin my project. Eventually she laid fifty-seven eggs, enough to rear a pure brood of the Bitterroots moths and provide stock for my experimental crosses. I slept well the rest of the night in spite of the cold.

These Bitterroots populations had been named "*kasloensis*" in the early 1900s, after the town of Kaslo in British Columbia where the first specimens were taken. The moths were thought to be a dark, nearly melanic, form of the Pacific Coast *euryalus* until Sweadner proposed their hybrid origin. Even current authors were uncertain of their taxonomic status, partly because the pattern of intergradation was geographically so broad instead of a small population of intermediates clearly bounded by "parental" forms, as was the case in the Sierra Nevada.

I planned to pursue three goals: (1) use computer-aided multivariate statistics to analyze wing patterns from a transect across the suspected zone of hybridization from Coeur d'Alene to Helena, the endpoints established originally by Sweadner; (2) rear and describe the life stages of pure *"kasloensis"* and compare these with *euryalus* and *gloveri*; and (3) make a series of experimental crosses between *"kasloensis"* and other *Hyalophora* to determine patterns of compatibility. These crosses would be based on the assumption that degree of compatibility would be a measure of genetic similarity. In this way I could characterize the genetic makeup of a regional population, and perhaps shed light on the historical origins of the hybrid zone. I knew from my Monitor Pass work, and from other published hybrid zone research, that the appearance of wild hybrids, even when analyzed with sophisticated statistical methods, does not necessarily indicate the true genetic makeup of an individual. For example, because of backcrossing and genetic recombination, a hybrid individual might appear to resemble one species but be genetically more like the other parent. Test crosses held the promise of at least indirectly revealing the makeup of genes controlling reproduction. My previous work had led me to believe that reproductive compatibility determined the width and structure of *Hyalophora* hybrid zones (the tension zone model) much more than ecological adaptations (the hybrid superiority/ ecological model), which were very similar in the hybridizing species, or wing pattern features, which are generally highly variable in hybrid zones and may be selectively neutral.

The Bitterroots project took longer than I anticipated and produced some surprising results. In 1997, after five years of fieldwork and about 120 experimental crosses, I finally published a monograph in the *Annals of Carnegie Museum* which I dedicated to Sweadner's original publication in the same journal. My work confirmed Sweadner's natural hybridization hypothesis, with my analysis of wing pattern variation closely matching his transect from Helena to Coeur d'Alene. Rather than a single zone of east–west intergradation, I discovered two additional hybrid zones, all separated from one another by high, rugged peaks. In addition, it was obvious that the history of interbreeding was much more complex than anyone had expected. Indeed, the history of all these populations might be the best way to summarize my work. The theoretical reconstruction that follows rests largely on published studies of the sequence of paleoclimates and corresponding plant communities during and following the Ice Age.

At the time of maximum Pleistocene glaciation, the genus *Hyalophora* probably existed as three distinct taxa: the West Coast ancestor of *euryalus,* confined to warmer coastal regions and the lower elevations of its present range; the ancestor of *gloveri,* occupying the Sierra Madre in Mexico (where it still resides) and reaching its northern limit in the southern Rockies, and isolated from the West Coast populations by the glaciated Sierra Nevada; and the ancestor of *cecropia,* in the southeastern part of North America, a known Ice Age refugium and current center of high plant diversity. An extensive Mississippi delta and barren sandy terrain isolated *cecropia* from the Rocky Mountains populations.

As *gloveri* reinvaded the northern Rockies at the end of the Ice Age, the larvae of its frontier populations probably fed on conifers, including mountain larch, in addition to willow and wild cherries. Conifer feeding may be an ancestral condition in *Hyalophora*; Sierra and Cascade *euryalus* feed on Douglas-fir. Mountain larch is common at elevations in the Bitterroots where "*kasloensis*" is found, but other known hosts are scarce. It probably feeds on larch here, but I haven't yet been able to confirm this.

Currently, the northernmost *Hyalophora* from Winnipeg and eastward in Canada and the Great Lakes region feed on the eastern larch (tamarack), a smaller tree that grows in bogs and swamps. The Great Lakes moths are a small, dark race once considered a separate species (*H. columbia*). A Canadian worker and I independently discovered that this form smoothly intergrades with the larger, wine red form of *gloveri* in the Canadian Prairie Provinces and northern Rockies. (Because the Great Lakes race was described first, the Rocky Mountains form is now technically *H. columbia gloveri.*)

Climatic warming also allowed the West Coast populations to advance northward, where they eventually met and hybridized with the Rocky Mountains *Hyalophora* in the Bitterroots. I believe this initial contact was between *euryalus* and the small, dark form (in formal taxonomy, *H. columbia columbia*), as evidenced by the relatively smaller size and dark coloration of "*kasloensis*," by a slightly higher compatibility when crossed to Great Lakes moths compared with Rocky Mountains populations, and by larval coloration in the Bitterroots, which more closely resembles the Great Lakes caterpillars. Subsequently, the small, dark, larch-feeding *Hyalophora* moved farther north and east to occupy its present range. The prairie pothole lakes of the Dakotas are remnant tamarack (larch) bogs. Both the moth and its favored plant community have moved northward with a changing climate.

The present-day contact between *"kasloensis"* and *gloveri* near Helena is secondary to the original episode of hybridization with the dark form, now displaced to the north and east, and may not be at present a region of extensive gene exchange. There is a rather abrupt change from the *"kasloensis"* form into the Rocky Mountains *gloveri* phenotype. This could be due to a partial barrier resulting from a scarcity of host plants caused by the rain shadow effect of the Bitterroots. Some degree of intrinsic genetic incompatibility may also account for the narrow zone of blending between the two forms.

In fact, I found that even between separate regions within *"kasloensis"* there was more infertility than I had seen in interpopulation crosses in other forms. This finding and other evidence support the concept of many separate populations of hybrid origin, each at one time isolated in an Ice Age refugium, where each achieved through natural selection a genetically different solution to the inherent incompatibility between the original hybridizing taxa. The paleobotanist Rexford Daubenmire has identified certain west-facing canyons in the Bitterroots as refugia historically warmed by coastal weather patterns. These canyons now support relict populations of plants whose main distribution is more coastal. *Hyalophora* might well have populated such refugia, especially during warmer interglacial periods in the Pleistocene. Godfrey Hewitt proposed such a model for the pattern of hybridizing crickets he studied in similar glaciated terrain in the Alps and Pyrenees. More recently, workers at the University of Idaho in Moscow have found a similar mosaic pattern of chipmunks of hybrid origin, lending credence to a model of initial hybridization followed by isolation and subsequent range expansion with secondary contact between populations. Incompatibility, arising during isolation, limits free gene exchange in these regions of secondary contact (for example, as seen in the inter-"*kasloensis*" crosses).

A separate and distinct hybrid population occurs north and east of Boise, Idaho. These moths are larger and more brightly colored than "*kasloensis*" and are probably the product of a separate post-Pleistocene contact between *euryalus* and the large, brightly colored Rocky Mountains form of *gloveri*. A third zone appears to be a remnant hybrid zone at the southern end of the Bitterroots where the present-day climate is too cold to allow host plants and *Hyalophora* to continuously breed over Lost Trails Pass.

My historical reconstruction of the events producing our

current *Hyalophora* species is only a best guess of the true phylogenetic history. This picture does fairly depict the many independent forces that shape species: changing climates and plant communities, the genetic constitution of interacting taxa, and the complexity of topography. Detailed DNA analyses now in progress will be a test of this model.

⚜

"JOHN, WHATEVER HAPPENED to Walter Sweadner"? I was calling my friend John Rawlins, curator of invertebrates at Carnegie Museum in Pittsburgh, to plan a visit to the museum. I needed to meet with the editor of the *Annals* to go over the final draft of my monograph, but I had also been thinking about writing a biographical article for *Carnegie Magazine,* a popular publication with articles relating to all the museum's branches: history, art, and natural history. Sweadner's life story would certainly have both historical and scientific significance.

"Mike, Walter Sweadner's life had a sad and tragic end. He died of cancer before he was even fifty, and just at the peak of his career here at the museum. He and Avinoff had just finished this big monograph on the *Karanasa* [a satyrid butterfly from the mountains of Tibet]. These bugs are kind of like your *Hyalophora*, a montane group that has lots of intergrades and hybrids—an impressive piece of work. First Avinoff died of a heart attack, and then Sweadner got cancer and died just before publication. Damned shame . . ."

"John, I didn't know any of this, but I always wondered why he hadn't published more. I'd like to write something up about him."

"I'll send you a copy of the *Karanasa* paper, and I think I know someone who can get you in touch with Sweadner's widow, if she's still alive. There's a daughter, too—living on the East Coast. I'll get back to you."

I asked John to look through the dark and dusty corners of the museum for any of Sweadner's papers. John had already boxed up and sent me dozens of Sweadner's specimens, including the "*kasloensis*" he collected in the Bitterroots. Most had a code number attached to them. Sweadner had carefully measured the shape of the hind wing eyespot to show the geographic pattern of intergradation from the narrow, comma-shaped eyespot of *euryalus* near Coeur d'Alene to the blunt, kidney-shaped spot near Helena that characterizes *gloveri*. He then mathematically calculated an index, based on the ratio of length to area. This kind of quantitative analysis, conveyed by Sweadner in a series of convincing

Walter Sweadner, a prolific worker in entomology at the Carnegie Museum of Natural History from the 1930s until his untimely death in 1951, developed a modern concept of the species and published the first quantitative analysis of a hybrid zone.

charts and figures, was extraordinary for its time. Sweadner's was the first hybrid zone paper published in English (following a German paper on hybridizing crows), and the first to use a mathematical index of "hybridity." Following standard practice for analysis of hybridization, I had used a package of multivariate statistics to similarly portray hybridization in the Monitor Pass study, as well as the soon-to-be-published "*kasloensis*" paper. Sweadner had done it all by hand, drawing on his engineering background.

I had originally hoped to find Sweadner's codebook with each specimen's eyespot "score," which I could then compare with my analysis, and perhaps even see if the structure of the hybrid zone had changed in sixty years. No such book had turned up, but now I wondered if any of Sweadner's personal notebooks existed, perhaps a diary or log of his Bitterroots trip. He traveled through rough country on bad roads and appears to have camped out more often than not. His base camp was on Lookout Pass, outside Missoula, Montana. Today weekend skiers sip cafe latte in comfortable lodges, but Sweadner probably slept in his Model A truck, which he converted into a portable field station, as an old newspaper photo shows. His diary would be fascinating reading.

In the meantime, I wrote to Marie Sweadner, Walter Sweadner's widow, having gotten her address from a friend of John's who knew her. About ten days later I received a letter from Kathy Sweadner, her daughter, a doctor and professor of medicine at Harvard Medical School. She was delighted that someone was interested in her dad's work and had encouraged her mother to receive my phone call.

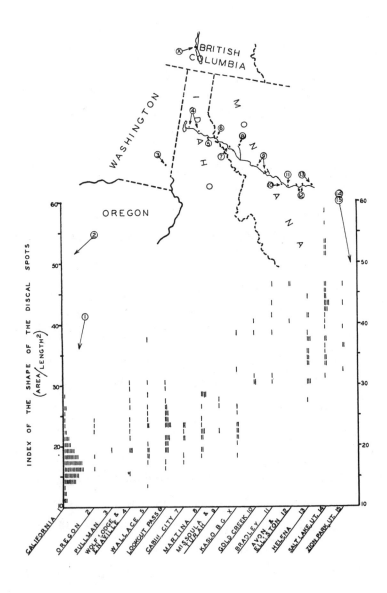

Marie had not talked to anyone about her husband's work for forty years and, being a private and somewhat shy person, was unsure how to respond to my request to meet and interview her.

I was nervous as I prepared to make the call. I had admired her husband for so long and had expended so much effort in elaborating his original insight that the emotional investment, long muted and unexpressed, came forward. "Hello, . . . yes, this is Marie Sweadner (she pronounced it *Sway-d-ner*)." Her voice was quiet but not timid, and I managed to convey my sincerity and good intentions. We quickly became comfortable talking to each other. "I don't have a lot of Walter's things, not things you'd probably be interested in," she said, "and I don't know much about his work, but I would be glad to meet with you."

My wife, youngest daughter, and I flew to San Diego and arranged to stay with friends. Marie lived just five minutes away. She greeted us warmly and at once I saw that she was

FACING PAGE:
Reproduction of Sweadner's analysis of eyespot shape as it changes across the *Hyalophora* hybrid zone in the Bitterroot Mountains. An s-shaped curve (as used to model hybrid zones) could be fitted to these data points. Courtesy Carnegie Museum of Natural History.

an amateur naturalist; her shelves were lined with wildflower and bird field guides. My wife and daughter played a little classical music together, we had a glass of wine and snacks and agreed we would all have lunch together, but first I wanted time alone to interview Marie. I thought a tape recorder might be intimidating, so I used a yellow legal pad and pencil to take notes instead. I came back the next day. At times I put down the pad and we just talked and laughed together, off the record. I later received warm letters of appreciation from both Marie and her daughter, who proudly showed off the article to her own children, who had never known their grandfather.

※

SEVERAL YEARS after I wrote the Sweadner article I was planning another trip to the Carnegie Museum to begin new research of speciation in the *Hyalophora* group using gene sequence data, to be generated in their new DNA lab. During a phone conversation, John Rawlins said he had found something of great interest to me: Sweadner's field notes from his 1932 Bitterroots trip. "I hadn't found it before because the title on the spine of the book was torn off," he said. "I had been looking for something else in the bookcase of field notes and there it was, filed out of sequence. It's quite long, and at the end are a lot of numbers. Maybe it's the codebook you were looking for." Once in Pittsburgh I had a hard time putting down the book to work on our new project. I soon learned to read Sweadner's handwriting, and while the specimen scoring code numbers were not there and I couldn't compare Sweadner's scoring methods with mine, the daily diary was extensive and very detailed. John agreed to have the book scanned so that I could leave the volume there and use a computer file to transcribe the text at my leisure.

Sweadner left on March 22, 1932, driving alone at age twenty-nine into country new to him. "Rolled along at 30 miles per hour over perfect roads through Iowa," he wrote on his third day. He had covered 435 miles, a good day's drive even today. "I find it very hard to write after having driven all day." Yet, each day he found time to write careful notes on the scenery and wildlife he encountered. He first drove to Utah, where he collected wild cocoons of *Hyalophora gloveri* and plant and animal specimens for the Carnegie Museum and University of Pennsylvania. I was surprised to learn how many local amateur and professional biologists he met in each region he visited. During his stay in Utah, with the aid of such guides, Sweadner was deeply impressed by the dramatic topography of the "Canyon Land" region.

> I arrived at Bryce Canyon about mid afternoon and used up a roll of film in what I believe will be a vain attempt to carry away a record of this fantasy in the rock. Only a color panorama camera could touch it. You come onto the rim of the canyon over a long stretch of almost level land forested with pine and cedar, and at this time of the year almost covered with snow. You burst forth from this to a chasm filled with spires, ridges and all sorts of grotesque forms in all the colors of the rainbow. The spires and ridges vary up to several hundred feet high and are so narrow at the base that you wonder how they remain erect. I started down the Navajo Trail which zig-zags down one of the talus slopes. I had difficulty getting over some places where landslides had wiped out the trail and was finally stopped about a quarter of the way from the bottom by deep snow and the fact that the rocks falling from the spires that rose on either side on me were falling too frequently and too close.

Sweadner met a variety of people—game wardens, sheep herders, miners, university professors, amateur butterfly collectors—and seemed to enjoy engaging each in conversation, often staying for a home-cooked meal. He made plans with a Boy Scout leader to collect the local *Hyalophora,* using as bait females he would supply as cocoons. At the beginning of May, Sweadner left Utah and drove north to the Bitterroot Range along the border between Idaho and Montana. After receiving a final shot of spotted fever serum as a precaution against tick bites, Sweadner made a base camp just west of Lookout Pass near the silver-mining town of Wallace, Idaho. After getting permission by the mine owner to use an abandoned cabin, Sweadner wrote:

> Thursday May 12—Spent most of the day exploring camp. Porcupines used my cabin last winter and have all the paper chewed off for about two feet above the floor. There are no windows in any of the cabins, they having been stolen along with everything that could be removed with a crowbar by the people from town. I managed to find two tables and a broken chair that can be repaired. Two *gloveri* and a *cecropia* emerged, so I built a large breeding cage.

And later: "It seems that in taking the cabin here, I have invaded the home of a porcupine. I have driven him out twice, but he persists. Today I belabored him with a club (a long one). Perhaps that will discourage him." Entries written over the following days indicate that Sweadner was not prepared for the long intervals of cold, rainy weather typical of the Bitterroots in late spring, but when the skies were clear he invariably set out to collect butterflies and plants.

Thursday May 26: The sun came out this morning long enough to encourage a few daring butterflies to take wing. I caught some fine ones. I took Graham's tin can along and collected plants also. I got some beauties. At the base of a rugged cliff, shaded by snowberry bushes there was a number of pure white shooting stars with black stamens. They are exquisitely beautiful. Later I found some real lilies, a greenish yellow veined with brown. And then high upon the ridge I found a pair of gorgeously beautiful pink orchids. I remembered reading about their rarity and the difficulty that the author had in finding them in a past *Nature Magazine*. And to top it all, I got caught in a *sleet* storm about three miles from camp. On the way back I found four more orchids. On account of the uncertainty of the weather with rain coming when you least expect it, I now put away dry wood I find in the car so I may be sure I can make a fire to cook the next meal.

His day typically involved setting out newly hatched female moths, each tied to a branch with a soft string (saturniid females remain quiet until mated), and recovering mated females and their mates from the previous day's trap line. Later in the summer he spent many hours feeding caged larvae from these crosses.

On June 4, his supplies apparently running low, he wrote: "When I reached Mullen I found no end of bad news awaiting me. The cocoons that Forbes was to send had been eaten by mice, news of a drastic cut in the Zoology Department budget, Dr. Williams going to South America this year rather than next, and last and most important no money till next week, with me having 82¢." A few days later, in seemingly good humor: "I just found out that cheese and crumbled 'Shredded Wheat' fried together over a slow fire makes a pretty good "omelette." The next day he "—went to Mullan but no money was waiting [at the post office] as I expected. I then performed the miracle of persuading a banker to cash a personal check, but anything may happen where they write their checks in pencil."

In spite of his hardships Sweadner's spirits remained high, buoyed by his intense interest in his moth work and the enjoyment he found in collecting specimens of new species in beautiful surroundings. Near the end of his fieldwork Sweadner joined a new acquaintance, an amateur collector named Heullemann (whose first name is never used) for a trip to a high mountain pass to collect butterflies.

Mr. Huellemann had been over the road, so I did not inquire as to directions. After we became lost in the Coeur d'Alene Mountains I found out that it was *24 years* ago that he was last over this way. We eventually reached Pritchard, but the road was steep, rough and just one dangerous turn after another. At Pritchard we entered the National Forest over a road that had been made from an old railroad bed by scraping just once. A bridge also had been washed out and we crossed the river on two lines of logs placed the width of the car apart. We arrived at Big Creek the end of the road shortly after noon and started the six mile climb to the peak. Mr Huellemann, who is 62 years old and does not weigh a hundred pounds, had a forty pound pack so we traded,

I taking his pack and my blanket roll. We had to wade the North Fork of the Coeur d'Alene River and I lost my footing and sat down, getting wet to the arm pits and soaking my blanket roll. Fortunately, I had forgotten to bring my camera, so it did not get wet. We wrung most of the water from the blanket, but they sure were heavy. The next three miles were some pull over a steep trail full of loose rock. At the water hole, Charlie Huellemann [the son], the lookout, met us with his donkey. Oh, what a relief.

Following a side trip to Glacier Park in northern Montana, where he "chased four toads and three bears [!] off the trail," Sweadner packed up his gear and his cages of caterpillars and returned to Pittsburgh. There are no diary entries on the return trip; perhaps he preferred to use the time to privately recall all he had experienced.

MARIE SAID she met Walter Sweadner after he had published the Bitterroots paper, and she didn't recall him talking about it. By this time he was involved in curating the Carnegie's

The intergrade form *H. "kasloensis"* found in the Bitterroots hybrid zone.

insect collection, especially the Lepidoptera, which he inherited from the legendary, and autocratic, W. J. Holland. Although
massive in scope it was in taxonomic disarray. He was joined in
this work by his supervisor and collaborator, André Avinoff, a
Russian émigré whose family once were frequent visitors in the
czar's palace. Avinoff was an intellectual, cultured in the Euro-
pean tradition and with a metaphysical facet to his otherwise

scientific approach to life. (His sister was the artist painting Roosevelt in Warm Springs when he died.) Sweadner came from more humble roots in Beaver, Pennsylvania, but went on to obtain degrees in both engineering and biology. Marie fondly recalled Avinoff coming over for dinner after working all day with her husband and staying late to play the piano.

There is a large foldout figure in Sweadner and Avinoff's *Karanasa* paper that attempts to present in n-dimensions, with lines and circles and tree branches drawn in artistic perspective, various aspects of the relationship among the *Karanasa* taxa: phenotypic, geographic, and phylogenetic. I have never been able to quite figure it out, but I'm sure that it represents aspects of both men's mutual interest in speciation and evolution and also their different approaches, one quantitative and analytical, the other abstract and multi-dimensional. (Of the two-dimensional diagram the authors lament: "One should really have some curved fourth-dimensional space postulated by the theory of relativity to work out a model of theoretical [taxonomic] inter-linkage.") What conversations those two must have had!

Sweadner died just as the three-dimensional structure of DNA was discovered and just as the renaissance in evolutionary biology was flowering. Dobzhansky's synthesis of evolutionary thought, *Genetics and the Origin of Species,* was published shortly after Sweadner's Bitterroots study, denying Sweadner the insights of this work, yet in his "*kasloensis*" paper Sweadner independently advocated reproductive isolation as a criterion defining species. Subsequent editions of Dobzhansky's book cited Sweadner for this modern concept of the species. Had Sweadner lived, I'm sure he would have contributed many more insightful studies in this rich environment.

CHAPTER EIGHT

The Species Problem
and the Problem with Species

A BIOLOGIST'S REALITY is the natural world, within which modern society exists in an unnatural, artificial environment that is supported at great cost in energy and resources. This philosophical premise seems so simple and obvious that scientists are often startled to be reminded that much of society sees nature as a sort of theme park largely confined to a few refuges—a fate awaiting the remaining wild areas yet to be conquered. Our food, water, and shelter ultimately derive from global nutrient and resource cycles flowing through ecosystems whose health depends on interactions among diverse plants and animals. In a tragic paradox, "primitive" peoples have a far greater appreciation of the critical need to protect biodiversity than urban sophisticates have. More ominously, the higher levels of government—where decisive response is most critical—are often the last to acknowledge impending environmental crises such as mass extinction or global warming.

Understanding the origin of biodiversity is basic to debating and resolving arguments about humankind's proper role in nature. Speciation is the fundamental process of incremental change in evolution producing biodiversity. For this reason, speciation and species concepts are more than just important philosophical and theoretical pursuits in academia; they should also be central topics in setting public policy in environmental law and conservation. For example, should we protect only those species currently defined in conservation law as populations able to interbreed, or should we recognize and protect unique and unusual subspecies, many of which also serve as indicators of the health of biological communities?

Many biologists have a personal and emotional attachment to certain species and taxonomic groups. I began this book by saying that the wild silk moths were my guides in studying nature. As I matured I learned to ask more sophisticated questions in ecology and evolution. The moths kept faith by revealing new and more challenging topics. Played out over the years, this harmonious question-and-response relationship, like an improvised Brubeck and Desmond fugue, has endured. A favorite species or group of species has become a supportive friend—indeed, a guide through the bewildering complexity of the insect world.

The species is the common currency among biologists in their work and communication. Basic questions in ecology, such as what regulates the distribution and abundance of organisms, must first be addressed by seeking to understand the evolutionary origin of adaptations. Are shared adaptations among similar species the result of common ancestry, or were they derived independently as convergent solutions to problems imposed by similar environments? What is the link between ecology and evolution as populations within a species become adapted to a diversity of environments over a geographic range? Does this genetic differentiation lead to reproductive isolation, and if so, how? Why do some species appear so uniform throughout vast ranges? Are their genomes similar because of common selection pressure or extensive gene flow, or is this uniformity more superficial, the product of homeostatic developmental systems that act as a buffer against both genetic and environmental variation? These are difficult and complex questions. The concept of the species in both theoretical and applied biology has remained controversial in spite of impressive gains in genetics, molecular biology, and computer modeling.

Ernst Mayr and other preeminent evolutionary biologists have noted the ability of indigenous peoples, isolated from our scientific culture, to give unique names to animals in their environment that nearly exactly match our formal taxonomic list of species. Genetic assays also support the concept of species as real biological entities—discrete units of biological diversity—not abstract constructs reflecting one culture's tendency to categorize. While nearly all scientists agree that the species concept is real when referring to populations in nature, agreement on a concept of species as evolutionary units has been more problematical. How does one define species boundaries among populations with significant geographic variation over space (horizontal evolution), or among a sequence of fossils as segments of time within ancestor-descendent lineages (vertical evolution)?

Darwin, lacking an understanding of genetics and therefore a clear idea of reproductive isolation, was impressed by geographical variation in nature and saw species as abstract endpoints of a continuum in both time and space. Speciation, as the basic mechanism of evolutionary change, was in his view gradual, directed by the mechanism of natural selection favoring any variation that better adapted an organism to its environment.

The "species problem" is part of the history of controversy among biologists in their attempts to classify biological diversity. Classification systems use both similarities and differences. Taxonomists constructing trees of relationships have traditionally defined major groups on the basis of a *shared* body plan, such as a bony spine and two pairs of fins or limbs for the vertebrates, and have distinguished classes within these groups on the basis of *differences*, such as type of skin (moist in amphibians, scaly for reptiles, etc.). The vertebrate body plan is "ancestral," and the distinguishing characters for amphibians, reptiles, and so on are "derived" with respect to the original, primitive vertebrates. The same methods have long been used for classifying species and genera, although at this level the character differences are increasingly detailed and subtle, and the classification process becomes more subjective and intuitive. Sexually reproducing animal species exist in geographically defined natural populations whose members we can count and observe in the wild. All other major groupings—genera, families, and above—are in this sense abstractions that nevertheless help us classify organic diversity. There are no standard conventions for dividing diversity into units; for example, defining how distinct a group of species must be to be recognized as a separate genus.

Some workers might prefer a few large genera, others many smaller genera or even subgenera.

With the formulation of the evolutionary synthesis, Dobzhansky, Mayr, and others used reproductive isolation as a means to define species because they saw it as an operational criterion, recognizing that while selection acts on the individual, the population—with its shared pool of genetic variation—is the unit of evolution. Sexual reproduction leads to a genetic cohesion in which interbreeding members of a population share the genetic programs that regulate their growth and development, and express adaptive traits favored by natural selection. The genetic integrity of species, and therefore also the very foundation of biodiversity, stems from reproductive isolation; until gene exchange is reduced below some critical level, two diverging species cannot pursue independent evolutionary fates.

DARWIN'S STUDY in Down House is a scene of comforting clutter, with open books, loose notes, sketches, specimens, and other odds and ends lying about as if the great thinker had just stepped into the next room. A velvet-covered rope is the only obvious security, and David Attenborough's recorded voice from the audio wand the only intrusion. No visiting biologist can resist the fantasy that Darwin might appear and invite his visitor to sit down to discuss the current status of his theory. Once brought up to speed on genetics, he surely would ask, "Is there a genetic mechanism that drives the origin of species? Are there unique speciation genes?" Even some of Darwin's most fervent contemporary supporters were troubled by the sterility and loss of vitality often seen in hybrids between domestic animal species. Given such differences between species, how could natural selection bridge the gap in fitness in the gradual evolution of one species into another in the wild?

The best answer would probably be structured around the distinction between pre- and postmating barriers to interbreeding. Premating barriers are any differences between two potentially interbreeding species that act before mating; the equivalent term "prezygotic" (preembryo) is often used. New species are thought to arise most commonly when related populations become geographically isolated through colonization or range fragmentation—perhaps as the result of climate change. Recalling the ability of strong selection to differentiate a species through the formation of character clines, even in the face of gene flow, we can appreciate that two recently isolated populations will soon become genetically distinct. Successful

reproduction involves an elaborate premating sequence of be-
haviors for locating and identifying a suitable mate within a
defined ecological setting. As the two populations separately
adapt to their new environments, their respective members
may eventually fail to recognize each other as potential mates
should their ranges again come together. Premating isolation
probably most often arises merely as a chance by-product of
some ecological adaptation, such as a shift in seasonality or
diurnal activity rhythm that fortuitously serves as a barrier
to mating only when the ranges of the two incipient species
overlap after a period of isolation.

If premating barriers do not arise in isolation, hybrids
produced when the two species again come into contact may
nevertheless be unfit. Postmating (postzygotic) barriers, such
as a failure of sperm to fertilize the egg or early death of the
hybrid embryo, typically evolve slowly as numerous small
genetic differences accumulate in the two diverging species.
Genes producing postmating isolation are adaptive in the
formation of the conspecific embryo but unfit in a hybrid
genome. Isolation in this case is an accidental by-product of
divergence in geographic isolation and is a phenomenon of
interaction between the two species resulting in developmental incompatibility only in the hybrid genome. Another

important distinction between pre- and postmating isolation is that natural selection cannot favor a strengthening of *post-*mating barriers, since such hybrids are by nature genetically less fit and will produce fewer offspring.

At this point in the discussion Darwin might ask, "Could postmating incompatibility in hybrids set the stage for the evolution of premating barriers that would eliminate the waste of hybridization?" Dobzhansky strongly favored this concept and promoted the evolution of isolating mechanisms as the last stage of speciation. Evidence from decades of study of natural populations has, surprisingly, only recently been summarized. Although not commonplace, a geographic pattern has emerged from experimental matings between certain species pairs (mostly *Drosophila* flies, but also other insects and some birds and amphibians) that have been shown in the lab to form unfit hybrids. Premating isolation is stronger in stock from areas where the ranges of the two species overlap than in stocks derived from geographically separated populations. The inference is that postmating incompatibilities in hybrids provided the basis in natural selection for the evolution of premating barriers. The evolution of such barriers to interbreeding, following Dobzhansky's model, is not, however, a mechanism of speciation. The two populations in all probability had already reached the status of separate species when they were geographically isolated; the origin, or refinement, of premating barriers was not an adaptive response to interspecific gene exchange, but only eliminated the waste of gametes in fruitless hybridization. If this interpretation is correct, the crucial question is: "Can premating barriers arise between incipient species that are exchanging genes and producing hybrids of somewhat reduced fitness, short of complete infertility or inviability?"

One reason hybrid zones are so intriguing is that they are natural breeding experiments that may answer just such questions. The apparent long-term stability of many hybrid zones seems to indicate that premating barriers do not easily evolve in these settings. Several reasons why this is so have been proposed.

First, the distinct boundaries on each side of typically narrow hybrid zones are evidence of restricted gene exchange. Most matings just outside the hybrid zone are between members of the parent species, and so the arena for natural selection favoring the origin of mating barriers is restricted to the boundary between each parental species and the hybrid zone.

Second, any alteration in mating behavior or physiology that might reduce hybridization would likely disrupt pure species breeding and be selected against. A mating signal (sound, pheromone, signaling behavior, etc.) in one sex is almost certainly based on a much different structure and physiology, and controlled by different sets of genes, than the corresponding receiver in the opposite sex. A dramatic yet functional shift in such a coadapted system would require simultaneous and compatible genetic change in both sexes— an unlikely event.

Third, the regime in natural selection most favorable to the origin of premating barriers would be that of highly unfit hybrids, yet this condition would further restrict gene exchange across the hybrid zone, isolating the parent species from the effects of hybridization. The more unfit the hybrids (the stronger the postmating barrier), the less likely that premating barriers would evolve.

In summary, reproductive isolation demarks the origin of new species, yet speciation is not a predictable or predetermined evolutionary mechanism. No single class of gene controls reproductive isolation. Selection typically does not favor the acquisition of prezygotic reproductive isolation for this property in itself; such isolation is an incidental by-product of an adaptation in another context, most likely occurring when the two diverging taxa are isolated in differing environments.

Premating isolation can be reinforced when hybrids are unfit, although this is not a universal phenomenon. The genetic integrity of a species can remain intact in spite of small levels of hybridization.

The "biological species concept" (BSC) rests on observing or experimentally demonstrating genetic isolation from close relatives, but it also implicitly assigns to each species an ecological niche to which it is uniquely adapted. This species concept is thus part of the post-Darwinian synthesis of genetics, ecology, and systematics.

When breeding experiments are impractical, taxonomists have used gaps in the variation of certain characters or traits to indirectly demonstrate reproductive isolation. When such gaps occur within a geographic region (no intermediates are observed), the two groups revealed by such analysis are assumed to be reproductively isolated species. Judging species status among geographically separate (allopatric) populations, however, requires a best guess based on experience. This "morphological species" concept dates back to Darwin's time, but modern taxonomists have improved its rigor using computers and multivariate statistics. Ecological traits, as well as structural and biochemical characters, are useful in such comparisons.

Conceptual advancement and technology are supremely synergistic in science, and so it has been in the development of the species concept. With the advent of computers and molecular genetics, some evolutionary biologists proposed an alternative to the isolation criterion for species. They criticized the biological species concept as impractical because it does not stress evolutionary history and is at times misleading as to true relationships. This group rightly pointed out the difficulty of using reproductive compatibility in defining geographically separated taxa, which in most cases neither interbreed in nature nor are able to be experimentally hybridized in the lab. Captive interbreeding might measure the success of hybrid embryos to develop, for example, but might not show how fit they would be in the wild or whether subtle differences in mating behavior or sex pheromones would isolate the two forms in nature.

Mutations are random and accumulate inexorably over evolutionary time. Many small mutations in DNA are masked from natural selection because they don't alter the way the DNA code is read or because the resulting novel structure of the protein product does not alter its function. These types of mutation are passed on through the generations. Modern DNA sequencing techniques have become remarkably automated, and taxonomists can now run computer programs that convert genetic differences into trees of relationship. The odds of unrelated groups independently acquiring the same pattern of mutations (i.e., base-pair substitutions) within long DNA sequences are vanishingly small.

Proponents of the "phylogenetic species concept" (PSC) have developed computer programs that statistically analyze variation in taxonomic characters to distinguish ancestral from derived traits (especially for DNA sequence data). The results are used in constructing phylogenetic trees. Branches of these trees, stemming from a common ancestor, are called clades, and this approach to determining relationships is called cladistics. The concept is phylogenetic because it generates a proposed genetic lineage through time.

Speciation is represented in the PSC as an abrupt dichotomy, with daughter species replacing their ancestral form. Any trait arising subsequent to the speciation event will be confined to one or the other daughter species. Species are formally defined as the smallest group of populations that uniquely possess such derived traits. This method avoids all the practical difficulties of demonstrating isolation. Reproductive isolation is implicitly assumed, giving cohesion to a species, but is not explicitly used to define the species. In fact,

reproductive compatibility is said to represent a shared ancestral trait and is therefore deemed inappropriate, by defi-
nition, in delimiting species. This point of view, not widely
shared by population geneticists, seems to assume that reproductive compatibility will persist as two prospective species
diverge—for example, as geographical isolates. Such a point
of view questions the relevance of experimental hybridization in taxonomic studies.

The PSC has problems and limitations. A process called
"lineage sorting" partitions the pool of genetic variation in
an ancestral species into populations of descendant species
through natural selection and the vagaries of chance mating
and local extinction. Cladistic analyses of different genes, independently affected by this process, may yield contradictory
"gene trees," each a variation of the true phylogenetic history. Computer programs based on statistical likelihood have
been developed to deal with all these sources of error and
generate "consensus" trees. Often a principle of parsimony
is used to determine which tree would require the minimum
number of mutations within a given gene to explain differences among related species. Choosing among alternative
trees and setting limits on variation in derived traits makes
defining species boundaries using cladistics more subjective

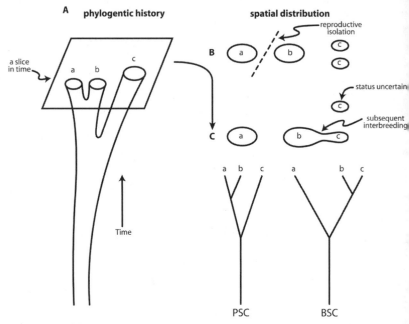

A. Basic to the controversy surrounding alternative species concepts is the distinction between a species' phylogenetic history—descent and divergence from an ancestor (represented by the branching diagram at left)—and the present-day distribution of populations (shown on the right by circles in B). Our current view of any species represents a slice in time of the dynamic process of speciation. In this example, analysis of DNA sequence data reveals under the phylogenetic species concept that **A** and **B** are sister species more closely related to each other than either is to **C**.

B. Although they are sister species, reproductive isolation now isolates **A** from **B**.

C. Subsequently, the range of **B** expanded, allowing interbreeding with **C**, with which it is still genetically compatible. Adherents to the biological species concept (BSC) would then place **B** and **C** as sister species in the absence of knowledge of the DNA-based phylogeny PSC. Depending on the length of separation (among other factors) the distinction between **B** and **C** would be lost if they were joined by a region of blending; if their hybrids were somehow unfit, a narrow hybrid zone would form and we might then judge them as separate species. A geographically isolated population of **C** would be of uncertain taxonomic status under the BSC. We could measure genetic cohesion only than might be supposed in a computer-driven analysis. The BSC and PSC are two central concepts in a field of debate that includes several other species concepts; my discussion here is therefore not comprehensive, but it does frame the debate.

After a period of surprisingly intense, even harsh, debate, the PSC has become the standard in taxonomy, especially for large groups of species and higher-level categories, for which the cladistic methods are most suited. But population geneticists object to what they see as the overzealous application of phylogenetic criteria, especially in cases where the acute resolving power of DNA techniques is used to designate as new species single populations uniquely possessing only minor genetic variants. A population geneticist might ignore these traits or list the populations as subspecies.

As ranges shrink due to environmental degradation, some intermediate blend zones disappear. With the blend zone eliminated, the populations at each end of what was once a continuum of genetic variation may now uniquely possess certain genetic markers, allowing the more dogmatic

---

by experimentally crossing members of separate populations. Lack of complete reproductive isolation among recently differentiated forms makes drawing species boundaries difficult under either species concept. The most informative view of these species would combine the perspective from both the PSC and BSC.

advocates of the phylogenetic concept to split old species into two or more new ones. Phylogenetic philosophy, through the default of extinction, produces new species by the hand of man rather than by natural genetic change!

A final criticism is that we cannot ignore the evolution of reproductive isolation, because this property gives genetic cohesion to the populations comprising a species and opposes the challenge that hybridization with closely related taxa poses to fitness. Genetic isolation has been shown (contrary to the views of cladists) to increase in effectiveness along with increased phylogenetic separation. The longer two species evolve along separate lineages, the more genetic differences they accumulate and the less successful their hybrids will be. Mate recognition traits (bird songs, pheromones, etc.) also diverge in this way after separation. Degree of reproductive isolation does reflect phylogenetic history, although certainly not as precisely as molecular evolution. While geographic barriers alone may initially isolate two incipient species, reproductive isolation based on genetic changes is an eventual consequence.

We cannot predict evolutionary fate, other than impending extinction as a result of our destructive habits. Climatic oscillation, as during the Pleistocene ice ages, causes the geographic ranges of organisms to retract and expand cyclically, leading to episodes of divergence in isolation followed by interbreeding and hybridization upon contact as ranges expand (such as seems to have occurred in the "*kasloensis*" intergrade *Hyalophora* in the Bitterroots). In such an environment, the potential to exchange genes with related populations would be critical in determining species status and evolutionary fate. What appear today to be distinct species occupying separate ranges could interbreed in the future, and therefore cease to evolve separately.

An example of climate change acting as an engine of speciation can be seen in a complex of hairstreak butterflies in the genus *Mitoura* (=*Callophrys* of some authors) recently studied by my old friend Art Shapiro and his students. Three currently recognized species (*nelsoni, muiri,* and *siva*) differ only subtly in adult color and pattern, but are more distinct in larval host plant and other ecological traits. As a group they inhabit the California Coast Range, the Cascades, and the Sierra Nevada foothills, which together form a ring around the Central Valley. The larvae eat members of the Cupressaceae (juniper, cypress, incense cedar), and in regions where any two hairstreaks occur together, each species feeds on a different host. These distinct populations tend to be isolated from each other as a consequence of their fidelity to their respective host plant, each of which is restricted to specific soil types. For example, Macnab's cypress grows in well-defined stands on serpentine and gabbro soils where incense cedar does poorly. Detailed mapping of the distribution of the butterflies shows that they occur in colonies. The different species are typically separated by only a few hundred yards or a few hundred feet in elevation, and usually by a few weeks in flight season. Courtship and mating occur only on the upper branches of the host plant, and neither sex disperses away from the colony.

Art demonstrated this for me one spring when he invited me to join him and his student Bruce Garvais, who was mapping out the various *Mitoura* populations. We met and drove to a serpentine community near my home in the Sierra foothills. Years ago in Art's ecology classes I had learned that more than two hundred plants are adapted to the high level of magnesium and heavy metals found in California's serpentine soils; on neighboring soils these plants would be poor competitors, but they thrive as endemics in their serpentine sanctuaries. When we spotted the digger pine and cypress in the distance, we knew we had reached the collecting site.

With nets in hand, Art and Bruce reached up and systematically sampled the Macnab cypress by tapping their nets against the upper branches. (I wasn't much help because I couldn't resist scanning the ground for the local horned lizard that also seems to favor serpentine soils.) Once or twice a female *Mitoura* flew away, tempting Art and Bruce to give chase (lepidopterists become inured to this ridiculous spectacle), hoping to see the butterfly settle on another cypress. Adults are best collected as they take nectar on flowers. The *Mitoura* species fly only in the spring, the foothills' short but glorious season of growth and reproduction and abundant wildflowers sandwiched between winter rains and the hot, dry California summer.

Their close similarity has made the taxonomy of these *Mitoura* species controversial among lepidopterists. Are they cryptic species, superficially similar but genetically quite distinct, or subspecies of one widely distributed species? Art was using modern molecular tools to determine their species status and perhaps end the controversy.

To increase the sensitivity of their analysis Art and his student Chris Nice used two independent measures of evolutionary divergence: electrophoresis, which measures changes in the composition of specific enzymes (coded for by nuclear DNA); and base sequence variation in specific genes in mitochondria (the maternally inherited organelles where the cell's metabolism takes place). The results were surprising; genetic differences among the three species were less than those typically seen among separate populations within a single butterfly species! Art and his students concluded that the three *Mitoura* forms must have diverged very recently and may be just at the point of becoming full species. They discount the alternative explanation—homogenizing gene exchange—in light of the effective ecological separation among the species.

Recent divergence is consistent with the geologic history of California. Confined to the Mojave Desert during the Ice Age, junipers have only recently colonized the area currently occupied by the three *Mitoura* species. As the climate stabilized about ten to twelve thousand years ago, each host plant occupied a preferred soil type. Evolution in the butterflies occurred most rapidly in genes controlling ecological adaptations, with each species adapting its flight season to coincide with the brief spring growth of its preferred host plant. By mating on their host, the three hairstreaks are reproductively isolated by their ecological traits.

When Matt Forister, another of Art's students, confined mixed pairs in cages, they readily mated, and all combinations yielded fully viable and fertile hybrids. The *Mitoura* complement the picture illustrated earlier by *Hemileuca* and *Hyalophora* and show that speciation can follow many different paths. Morphology, ecological traits, and reproductive isolation often evolve independently and at different rates as daughter species diverge during the speciation process.

Hemileuca nuttalli and *H. eglanterina* are sibling species in their superficial similarity but are strongly isolated by pheromone differences and mating flight times. They don't hybridize successfully in nature or in the lab. All three *Hemileuca* species have extensive distributions, and *eglanterina* especially is an ecological generalist in host plant choice. *Hyalophora euryalus* and *H. gloveri* are very distinct in appearance in all developmental stages, yet are not reproductively isolated and hybridize easily in nature and in cages. When stock from outside the hybrid zone is cross-mated in the lab, hybrid females are viable but sterile; within the hybrid zone intergrade females are fertile. Both *Hyalophora* species are extreme generalists and occupy a wide diversity of plant communities throughout their ranges. By various measures it appears that the *Hemileuca* and *Hyalophora* species are phylogenetically well differentiated, whereas the three *Mitoura* species have indistinct taxonomic boundaries and are isolated by subtle but effective ecological factors, not by the kinds of intrinsic genetic differences that produce hybrid sterility in the other genera.

This unique study in Shapiro's lab applied aspects of both the PSC and the BSC. It employed a cladistic analysis of molecular data, although no phylogenetic tree emerged due to the lack of genetic differentiation among the nominal species. The three species are best defined, each as a reproductive community, by the BSC in terms of observations on mating behavior and natural history traits, and by experimental hybridization. Most speciation studies are not as successful in using such a multidisciplinary approach.

Unfortunately, as species concepts continue to be debated, each group tends to ignore the other roughly along the lines of taxonomists (who apply a phylogenetic species concept to catalogue biodiversity) and population geneticists (who are interested in speciation as genetic and ecological processes). I suspect that part of the conflict erupts from a philosophical difference in portraying the daunting diversity of life, and not just in the details of species definitions. The phylogenetic group stresses the objective, computer-generated tree of relationship, where each branch arises from the dichotomy of a speciation event, one species giving rise to two new ones. Although a somewhat dogmatic view, over long geological spans of time this may be an accurate picture.

Population geneticists see species as loose assemblages of interbreeding populations in which reproductive barriers between related forms may be incomplete, leading in some cases to fuzzy species boundaries. The emphasis here is on genetic processes that produce and maintain genetic variation within species and limit the exchange of genes between species. Incomplete reproductive isolation might seem to challenge the BSC if interpreted too literally. Most population geneticists and those systematists employing the BSC judge species in terms of the genetic integrity or cohesion of populations. Modern DNA assay techniques allow us to show that the gene pool of populations, including critical genes controlling development and reproduction, usually remains intact despite occasional interspecific hybridization. Even hybrid zones, whose sharp borders are maintained by selection, can be seen as a kind of genetic filter or barrier limiting the degree of gene exchange outside these areas of interbreeding.

A cooperative approach in which each school helps identify interesting problems of species boundaries (such as hybrid zones) would be ideal. The phylogenetic approach promises to more accurately reveal past evolution; the population genetics approach reveals how genetic diversity is partitioned at present. We cannot afford these jurisdictional squabbles in a time of impending threat to global biodiversity.

CHAPTER NINE

The Fire

IT STARTED along U.S. Highway 395 just below Monitor Pass, but I didn't want to ask anyone the cause. It began in the fall, but I didn't visit the area until the following spring. Perhaps a spark from a chainsaw or a tossed cigarette ignited dry grass and fallen pinyon needles, which quickly flamed up beyond any hope of initial control. The fire burned a broad swath of hillside along the highway up the eastern slopes of Monitor Pass, from about five thousand feet to about seventy-five hundred. Only blackened skeletons of mature pinyon remained. All smaller growth, even mature sagebrush and tough, hardened bitterbrush, was reduced to ash. In the little canyon leading up to the pass from the highway the fire burned and charred the larger willows and cottonwoods until the vegetation close to the stream proved too lush to ignite in what must have been a very fast moving fire. The upper limit of devastation was just below the pull-off at seventy-five hundred feet where I have always placed my moth traps. Here, where moisture collects in the rock slide of basalt boulders, grow thick stands of bitter cherry and western chokecherry. I could always count on collecting a good series of males provided a cold storm did not blow through. If the fire crew had not fought the fire from the road just here, this population of unique hybrids would have perished. Downslope and around a bend in a steep-walled canyon the isolated stand of white fir and Jeffrey pine survived, as did the little population of mountain beavers (*Aplodontia*)—not a true beaver, but a relict rodent family whose evolutionary zenith has passed.

But so much else was lost. Rain falls only occasionally in the summer here; the green season is spring. The rough and rocky landscape is blanketed by the soft bloom of lemon yellow bitterbrush, and sagebrush meadows are streaked with splashes of wildflowers in pinks, reds, and orange. In their center, where snowmelt forms temporary ponds, wild iris adds a deep blue and attracts evening hummingbird moth pollinators. By late summer growth has stopped, seeds have matured, and the brown leaves of annual plants and rocky soil give the misleading impression of a sparse landscape. In fall the crop of pinyon nuts attract noisy flocks of pinyon jays and Clark's nutcrackers. Ground squirrels by day and deer mice by night harvest what the birds miss. The entire community seems centered on this Thanksgiving feast of pinyon nuts. Few nuts are left to germinate, and this may be one reason for the notoriously long postfire regeneration time for this region. (In Nevada and Utah, such countryside is known as "pinyon-juniper woodland," but no Great Basin species and only occasional Sierra juniper mix with pinyon in this region of the east slope.) Postfire soil moisture is very low when there are no roots or shade to retain rainfall, and nonnative annual grasses (often planted after a fire!) outcompete pinyon seedlings for water. Pine nuts are dispersed not by the wind but by pinyon jays, which place them in caches to be retrieved during the winter. The few nuts dropped or forgotten may germinate as colonizers. Some biologists think this is the dispersal mechanism by which pinyon and other pines colonized the isolated Nevada mountain ranges. Yet, even with healthy stands nearby, natural restoration of the pinyon community after a fire will require decades, probably a half century.

Man-made fires—in the wrong place at the wrong time, and too severe and too frequent—destroy nature but also steal from it time, time to reinvade, to restore, and to regenerate. Lightning, the natural fire-starter, tends to strike the barren peaks or nearby solitary pines. Here, above the stands of pinyon, the soil moisture is higher and fires are harder to start.

I thought about the near loss of the heart of the *Hyalophora* hybrid zone and convinced myself that I wasn't being selfish in my personal anguish. The blending of Sierra and Great Basin has spawned and supported this unique showcase of evolution that I was privileged to discover in my short lifetime. It certainly would have been a personal loss; my pain on seeing the cost of the fire was deep and sincere. I had enjoyed so many trips to Monitor Pass that I had come to view the genetic phenomenon of the hybrid zone as a permanent fixture of the landscape—as enduring as the surrounding peaks and valleys. If the fire had destroyed the moth population, I mused, would a reinvasion of this region reconstitute a hybrid zone, or is such an outcome in the game of population genetics unique to the post–Ice Age environment?

Following my drive up the burned mountainside, I stopped near the summit and hiked to the aspen grove to revisit the campsite where I did my *Hemileuca* study thirty years ago.

In the cool shade of the aspens I took off my hiking shoes and sank my toes in the dry, gravelly dark soil, walked a few paces, and remembered how I had loved the feel of the powdery clay along the edge of Erroll's driveway. I looked back at my footprints and laughed that this one part of me hadn't changed. Looking down the hill I couldn't see the old tracks I had once followed up to my campsite; the sagebrush and lupine had at last grown over them. As for my footprints, I knew that the first good rainstorm of summer would wash them away. And that is as it should be.

BIBLIOGRAPHY

GENERAL READING

Edey, M. A., and D. C. Johanson. 1989. *Blueprints: Solving the Mystery of Evolution.* Boston: Little, Brown. A concise history of evolutionary theory in a conversational, narrative style co-written by the discoverer of the famed "Lucy" fossil. Each chapter covers the contributions of a key researcher.

Himmelman, J. 2002. *Discovering Moths: Nighttime Jewels in Your Own Backyard.* Camden, Me.: Down East Books. A nature writer's personal account of his fascination with moths, their natural history, collecting, photography, etc. Many color photos.

Mayr, E. 1991. *One Long Argument: Charles Darwin and the Genesis of Modern Evolutionary Thought.* Cambridge: Harvard University Press. A concise paperback detailing the five theories underlying Darwin's concept of evolution.

Pielou, E. C. 1991. *After the Ice Age: The Return of Life to Glaciated North America.* Chicago: University of Chicago Press. A reconstruction of the changing climate following the Ice Age and the response of biological communities as they recolonized North America.

Schoenherr, A. A. 1992. *A Natural History of California.* Berkeley: University of California Press. The current standard reference covering California; an excellent resource for the serious naturalist.

Smith, G., ed. 2000. *Sierra East: Edge of the Great Basin.* Berkeley: University of California Press. A comprehensive natural history for this unique region.

Storer, T. I., R. L. Usinger, and D. Lukas. 2004. *Sierra Nevada Natural History.* Berkeley: University of California Press. A recent revision of this classic natural history; many new photographs.

Trimble, S. 1993. *The Sagebrush Ocean: A Natural History of the Great Basin.* Reno: University of Nevada Press. Coffee table format with beautiful photographs and engaging text.

Tuskes, P., J. Tuttle, and M. M. Collins. 1996. *The Wild Silk Moths of North America.* Ithaca: Cornell University Press. The standard reference for the natural history of North American saturniid moths; extensive bibliography.

Waldbauer, G. 1996. *Insects through the Seasons.* Cambridge: Harvard University Press. Informal account of the author's research on the ecology of the cecropia moth and other saturniids.

Wilson, E. O. 1992. *The Diversity of Life.* New York: Norton. A personal and philosophical plea by this preeminent writer to save the planet's natural communities.

SELECTED REFERENCES

Avise, J. C. 1994. *Molecular Markers, Natural History and Evolution.* New York: Chapman and Hall.

Breeden, R. L., ed. 1979. *America's Majestic Canyons.* Washington, D.C.: National Geographic Society.

Collins, M. M. 1984. Genetics and Ecology of a Hybrid Zone in *Hyalophora* (Lepidoptera: Saturniidae). *University of California Publications in Entomology* 104:1–93.

———. 1991. Speciation: A review of concepts and studies with special reference to Lepidoptera. *Journal of Research in Lepidoptera* 30(1–2):45–81.

————. 1997. Hybridization and speciation in *Hyalophora* (Insecta: Lepidoptera: Saturniidae): A reappraisal of W. R. Sweadner's classic study of a hybrid zone. *Annals Carnegie Museum* 66:411–455.

————. 1997. Walter Sweadner and the wild silk moths of the Bitterroot Mountains. *Carnegie Magazine* 63(7):20–25.

————. 2004. Interactions between *Saturnia* and *Antheraea:* Convergence or a Million Years of Stasis? *News of the Lepidopterists' Society* 46:116–118.

Collins, M. M., and P. M. Tuskes. 1979. Reproductive isolation in sympatric species of dayflying moths (*Hemileuca*: Saturniidae). *Evolution* 33:728–733.

Collins, M. M., and R. D. Weast. 1961. *The Wild Silk Moths of the United States: Saturniidae.* Collins Radio Co. Available from BioQuip entomology supplier.

Cowles, R. B. 1977. *Desert Journal.* Berkeley: University of California Press.

Coyne, J. A., and H. A. Orr. 2004. *Speciation.* Sunderland, Mass.: Sinauer.

Ehrlinger, J. R., L. A. Arnow, T. Arnow, I. B. McNulty, and N. C. Negus. 1992. Red Butte Canyon Research Area: History, flora, geology, climate, and ecology. *Great Basin Naturalist* 52:95–121.

Harrison, R. G., ed. 1993. *Hybrid Zones and the Evolutionary Process.* Oxford: Oxford University Press.

Howard, D. J., and S. H. Berlocher, eds. 1998. *Endless Forms.* Oxford: Oxford University Press.

Jaeger, E. C. 1965. *The California Deserts.* Stanford: Stanford University Press.

Krutch, J. W. 1955. *The Voice of the Desert, a Naturalist's Interpretation.* New York: Sloan.

Lowe, C. H. 1977. *Arizona's Natural Environment.* Tucson: University of Arizona Press.

Moore, D. W. 1999. *The Nature of Madera Canyon.* Tucson: Friends of Madera Canyon.

Nice, C. C., and A. M. Shapiro. 2001. Population genetic evidence of restricted gene flow between host races in the butterfly genus *Mitoura* (Lepidoptera: Lycaenidae). *Annals Entomological Society of America* 94:257–267.

Olin, G. 1994. *House in the Sun*. Tucson: Southwest Parks and Monuments Association.

Otte, D., and J. A. Endler, eds. 1989. *Speciation and Its Consequences*. Sunderland, Mass.: Sinauer.

Raby, P. 2001. *Alfred Russel Wallace: A Life*. Princeton: Princeton University Press.

Remington, C. L. 1968. Suture-zones of hybrid interaction between recently joined biotas. *Evolutionary Biology* 2:321–428.

Rubinoff, D., and F. A. H. Sperling. 2002. Evolution of ecological traits and wing morphology in *Hemileuca* (Saturniidae) based on a two-gene phylogeny. *Molecular Phylogenetics and Evolution* 25:70–86.

Sperling, F. A. H. 2003. Butterfly molecular systematics: Species definitions to higher-level phylogenies. *In Butterflies: Ecology and Evolution Taking Flight*, ed. C. Boggs, W. Watt, and P. Ehrlich, pp. 431–458. Chicago: University of Chicago Press.

INDEX

The abbreviation *pls.* refers to color plates, and page numbers in italics refer to figures.